"Fern took me to find Gene and to know the hopeful future he found. Her conversations with him are life, contact, love, infinite, human, important, and haunting."

CHARLES WALKER
Former Astronaut
and President,
National Space Society

"Candid and fascinating.... Not only the great company of Gene's admirers will be in Yvonne Fern's debt, but also all people interested in a remarkable television phenomenon and the personality and mind that made it possible."

DR. CHARLES MUSÈS,
Mathematician, Philosopher, and Coeditor
with Joseph Campbell of
*In All Her Names: Explorations
of the Feminine in Divinity*

"When Gene Roddenberry gave the world Star Trek, he opened the minds and hearts of more than one generation to new ways of seeing and perceiving the human endeavor in this complex universe. It is wonderful to have such a delightful book about him."

MADELEINE L'ENGLE
Author of
A Wrinkle in Time

"I haven't had to think so hard since Stephen Hawking's *A Brief History of Time.*"

WILLIAM E. HAYNES
Astronaut Systems Manager for
the Skylab Space Station

"Brilliant! No one can claim to know Gene Roddenberry without reading this book."

ERNEST C. OVER
Gene Roddenberry's Personal Assistant

GENE RODDENBERRY

PORTRAITS OF AMERICAN GENIUS

We are a people.
A people do not throw their geniuses away.
And if they are thrown away, it is our duty
as artists and as witnesses for the future
to collect them again for the sake of our children,
and, if necessary, bone by bone.

Alice Walker

Gene Roddenberry

THE LAST CONVERSATION

Yvonne Fern

FOREWORD BY ARTHUR C. CLARKE

UNIVERSITY OF CALIFORNIA PRESS   BERKELEY LOS ANGELES LONDON

University of California Press
Berkeley and Los Angeles, California

University of California Press, Ltd.
London, England

Library of Congress Cataloging-in-Publication Data
Fern, Yvonne, 1947–
  Gene Roddenberry : the last conversation : a
dialogue with the creator of Star Trek / Yvonne
Fern : foreword by Arthur C. Clarke.
    p. cm.—(Portraits of American genius : 2)
    ISBN 0-520-08842-5
    1. Roddenberry, Gene—Interviews.
    I. Roddenberry, Gene. II. Title. III. Series.
  PN1992.4.R55F47 1994
  791.45'0232'092—dc20   94-6531
                                            CIP

Printed in the United States of America
9 8 7 6 5 4 3 2 1

For Majel

CONTENTS

F ew men have left a finer legacy than Gene Roddenberry. At a dark time in human history, *Star Trek* pro-
moted the then unpopular ideals of tolerance for dif-
fering cultures, and respect for all life forms—without
preaching and always with a saving sense of humor. We can
all rejoice that Gene achieved professional success and world
respect. There is a sad irony in the fact that he entered the
Undiscovered Country just when the eagerly awaited movie
of that name was about to be released, but it gives me great
satisfaction that he lived to see so many of his ideals trium-
phantly accepted.

Although Yvonne Fern met Gene Roddenberry toward
the end of his life, it is obvious that she got to know him very
well indeed. I am delighted that she has written such a per-
ceptive book about him.

Gene and I had a warm relationship for more than twenty years, and I wish Yvonne's thoughtful portrait of Gene Roddenberry all the success it deserves. I'm sure this will be guaranteed by the legions of intelligent people who will want to read it.

Arthur C. Clarke, Sri Lanka, October 18, 1993

There is a sense in which time is always present as space. Quantum physicists and astronomers describe the time/space differential as the result of space travel at (or near) the speed of light. And yet the point at which space becomes time (and the reverse) exists as a constant in everyday life as the verb "to be."

"Where *are* you?" carries within it the word "now."

"What time *is* it?" implies both "now" and "here, in this space."

Among the many unanswerable questions I have pondered over the years was one posed by my son when he was about six years old. When asked: "What time is it?" he replied, "What time is what?"

This is the very heart of the spiraled and unending quest of Gene Roddenberry: "What does it mean *to be?* In this time, in this space, who are we?" His struggle to answer these questions is a tale of time slippage and alternate space, a delicate and determined unraveling of current quantum theory—physics to metaphysics and back again.

Quantum theory gives rise to the postulation that the universe consists of several linear, simultaneously active dimensions which coexist as interweaving patterns of timespace that are not relative to each other except at "weak points" where they meet. It indicates that several worlds may cohabit the same space at the same time, and remain unperceived because the "fabric" of one dimension is atomically dissimilar to the pattern of another. Only at random points of exceedingly low probability could the non-time–non-space between these dimensions ever be traversed. Gene's quest was to somehow leap over that chasm called "between"—to discover the random, the serendipitous, the luminous light shining through the tight woven cloth of our timespace reality; to break through, as it were, and leave his swaddling clothes behind.

Gene Roddenberry did not believe in time. He never spoke of the future in the future tense, to me. It was always, "the future is," not "the future will be." He saw it. It was present, within him. This is perhaps what is meant by the word "visionary," a word that was attached to him so often and for so long that it became a credential: Gene Roddenberry, Visionary. And it was not so much the creative effort to display what he saw, as the absolute conviction that he saw it, that is responsible for the stunning impact Gene has had on American culture. Star Trek is a household name, not merely because the television programs and movies are entertaining enough to engage the capricious attention of the viewing public, but because Star Trek speaks to the fundamental longing of the human race to *be*, to survive, and to survive happily into the future.

Gene

Gene Roddenberry's favorite description of humanity was "a child race." He believed that in the great cosmic scale of evolution, we were in the sandbox. Sometimes he changed that description to "an adolescent species"; other times, he equated our level of development to that of ten-year-olds. Whatever the metaphor, it was clear to him that to reach maturity as a species we must rely on something he felt was bred in our bones: goodness. It is that simple, and that complex. Perhaps the very reason for its magnetism is the fact that Star Trek has a message we have all heard before, and believed and tried, until it got too hard, or didn't work, or didn't appear clever enough to others. Until we grew up just a little too far past a luminous infancy, and not far enough into the sagacity of experience. Star Trek reaches into the kindergartens and kitchen tables of our minds and says: To survive, you must be good. There is such a thing as goodness. It is the hallmark of the human race. Believe in it.

From what perspective Gene arrived at that conclusion, it is difficult to determine. Sometimes he would say that he was "just a guy," that what he now thought was the product of many years of thinking. At other times, he would hint at a more metaphysical reason for his views, let slip something that he refused to explain. Most of the time, he would simply say "I don't know," a phrase he felt was the beginning of the answer to everything, the first commandment in his particular branch of ontology. He did feel, consistently, that he had an obligation to find answers.

Millions felt that he did. When Gene, by some self-engendered quantum leap, entered the outer reaches of a future dimension he called Star Trek, and found it wondrous, he did his best to bring that wonder into focus for others. He created a television show of the same name, not to depict the details of that future, but to demonstrate what it would take to get there. He built a bridge to tomorrow with the materials of today: curiosity, tolerance, openness, intelligence, discipline, daydreams, a willingness to help, technology, love, determination, and courage. All those things exist within us, he said. Use them.

His job, he so often said, was to daydream—and to return from the world of dreams to the life he led as "just a guy," and explain it to others.

Gene's vision, often interchangeable with a philosophy called Star Trek, confirms human impulses and early teaching; it preserves a certain naivete. It replaces the confidence and loyalty we once as a nation gave to our leaders, when once, we actually believed they were Kirks and Picards. Star Trek insists that if men and women of conscience sit at a round table, there will be knights, both male and female— there will be Camelot. Gene Roddenberry's Star Trek looks at the founding of nations, governments, and cultures of the future the way our forefathers did, with liberty and justice for all. It is a very old-fashioned television show, about an incredible future that depends on the ability to keep learning from mistakes—to say that even if the United States of America does not work the way it was meant to, the United Federation of Planets will. Or, that it will work better. Star Trek upholds Jeffersonian principles.

It also holds sacred a natural property of childhood: daydreams, insisting that if you believe in fairies, Tinkerbell will live. Or rather, if you believe in other life forms, you will look for them, build space stations and spaceships, and find ways to explore the galaxy. If you find them, you will have each made a wondrous discovery in each other. If you don't, you will find yourself part of a spacefaring culture, with a whole universe of possibilities to discover, and a whole history of whatever it took to get you there—and that in itself will point the way to further discovery. Either way, you will win. You will be on a journey.

Among many extraordinary things about him were certain habits of childhood kept, by design or innocence, within him, and yet he never remained a boy. He was very definitely a man, an adult of the species he was wont to call "child"—or perhaps of some other species altogether. Although in poor health during our entire friendship, and declining daily, he was a powerfully present man, a contradictory measure of wisdom and stubbornness—a paradoxical and amorphous mixture of freedom and constraint.

In his vision of the future, Gene pushed the principles of equality a little farther forward. In Star Trek equality is kinetic, quick, and real. It is not equal opportunity, but equal reality. It means that everyone's stomach *is* full, not potentially full; and that everyone's home is a decent place to live. It has a lot to do with the verb "to be." Or as Gene would often remark, "We are on a journey to keep an appointment with *whatever we are.*" Equality means, in Star Trek, that there is no equal pay for equal work—there is no pay for any work, because one works for the love of it and no other reason. Everyone's real job, according to Gene, is to explore what it means to be human; to refuse to accept what we perceive as the limits of the human mind; to traverse every possible dimension of outer space and discover what's out there; and to travel every possible level of intradimensional mind space and uncover what's in there.

To Gene, the greatest praise was the word "human" and the greatest condemnation was interference—to violate the inner space of someone else, to not leave him alone to dream his dreams, or not leave her alone to live her life. Inherent in his philosophy is the Prime Directive, the principle of noninterference on which the world of Star Trek depends. Proposing that maxim, he challenges in his shows the philosophical dialectic between help and hindrance, between personal ethics and cosmic morality. His greatest challenge was to determine how the inviolate aloneness of each human person could interact not only with other humans, but with machines and other lifeforms when, and only when, the human race takes its final leap into maturity. He was an agnostic contemplative, whose favorite meditation was the problem of how to form a peaceful, fluid, interconnective cooperative system of peaceful coexistence, while retaining a forceful self-identity; or, put more simply, how to meaningfully share who we are with others and still remain intact.

He made a lot of mistakes, he said, and took pleasure in pointing them out as milestones of achievement. To recognize mistakes, he felt, was the greatest progress anyone could make.

Gene and I shared very little in terms of experience. He was exactly my father's age. Having been born outside Pearl Harbor just after a war in which Gene flew eighty-nine missions as a U.S. Army Air Corps pilot in the Pacific, I am certain that my existence on this planet is related to his—that we shared a direct connection. My childhood was filled with stories of men like him, men who at the time the stories were being told were busy trying to forget what had engendered them. But not Gene. He needed to understand everything. He would exhibit such tenderness for the human race that when I asked a question like "How does that relate to your having killed so many of them?" he would plunge into a quest for an answer as if his own life depended on it.

We shared almost nothing of personality. His personality fluctuated according to circumstance, for reasons that he addresses in this book. His character remained the same: honorable, honest, and true. We met in the last few months of his life, and yet we spent more time talking together about the things that mattered most to him than he had with many others whom he had known for years. He insisted on it. He brought me home to his house, to his family, so that I would have no chance to mistake him for a television producer, or any other label that public life necessarily imposes. And as our relationship grew, he brought me inside him, to a place I can only describe as curiously like home. In some ways, this was a disadvantage. I cannot now, nor have I ever been able to see him from the outside in. I do not even know what color his eyes were. From the inside, from my perspective, they were blue, brown, gray, violet, green, hazel, and black—the colors of humanity. In other ways, this intense isolation allowed for the one thing that he wanted most: contact. Our connection was secluded and confined, the product of the last few months of a man's life. What he said, what he did, what I saw, in that very circumscribed time and space, is all I can offer.

But we were, as Gene said more than once, of the same species, he and I—with a penchant for camouflage, a horror of intrusion, a fascination with inner and outer space, and a certain relativity factor in which nothing was constant except that which we meant when we said "I." We wrote part of this book together, talked until he could no longer speak, and communicated for much longer than that. He made requests of me on his deathbed, told me his most well-kept secret, entrusted to my care what he loved most. He called me "changeling"; I called him "Sister Mary Gene." We both knew who was whom. We recognized each other. I don't know why he first agreed to do this book, before he knew me. He said once that it was a letter I had written him. Another time, he insisted that it was his own idea.

I know why he agreed to do it after we had met. And when he became aware inside that he was dying, his revelations became more urgent. The closer he grew to his final hour, the more he told me—sometimes in a word, sometimes one short sentence at a time. "Write about Majel," he said once when I thought he was sleeping. "Explain about Hitler," he said another time, giving me permission to write about something we were wondering whether to include or not. "Go to the studio . . . find Bob Justman . . . tell Leonard . . . Spock . . . Majel . . ."

And then he was gone.

We kept each other a secret, except from a very few. He feigned interest in me as a woman to his male friends. I pretended I did not know him well, after he died. I don't know why we did those things. There was no reason to. We just did. Perhaps it was because what we shared most deeply was an access to a personal dreamworld, the preservation of which superseded any necessity to dispense facts. Or it may have been just that instinctive rejection of interference, however innocuous it might have been. If there is one truth I can state unequivocally, it was that he was a far more private man than any of his interviews, speeches, or public activities would seem to indicate.

When he died, I went to some of those whom he called intimate friends, men he had told me understood something inside him that others could not. Of those, I interviewed only a few before I realized that it was a mistake. This book was

Gene

intended to be the result of primary contact, and, as it began
that way, I felt it should continue that way. It was also a
mistake for another reason. The group of men he called intimates were part of a generation that, as one of them told me,
"toughs it out." Some of the questions I asked were not the
kinds that would allow the pain of his death to stay decently
beneath the surface, and so, with great respect, courtesy,
kindness, and a sincere wish to help, his friends did not answer them. They would say, to a man, as if he had not died,
"Well, that's something Gene has to answer."

This is not because they did not know the answer. It was
because they did not know me. And it was a reticence of such
touching nobility, I would like to pay tribute to it here. I
thank them for the answers they did provide, and I honor
those they did not. There was one exception to this: Robert
H. (Bob) Justman, whom I am as honored to call friend as
Gene was. Bob put aside his own grief to contribute his understanding of Gene to this book. And, as it turned out, he
gave the same answers to my questions as Gene had. In the
end, I decided to incorporate very little secondary information. It is not that kind of book. It is a book about the beginning of self-revelation, cut short by death.

These were the last interviews Gene Roddenberry gave,
the last extended conversations he had. They represent his
latest thinking and—equally important according to his own
equation—his latest feeling. Do they define him? No. Nothing does. They do paint a portrait of something inside him,
something that continues to touch millions of people every
day.

I wish I could write much more of what Gene told me—
so much is beautiful, so much is brilliant, so much is revolu-

10   tionary. But I cannot. Some promises can be broken: those extracted unfairly, those that violate a more sacred trust, those made in ignorance. But this was not one of those promises. Gene gave me twenty years' grace. If I feel, in 2011, that the time is right, there will be another book.

For now, this one must suffice.

Gene

Worlds shrink as they expand, I remember thinking, walking across the lot at Paramount Pictures, on my way to first contact, as it is called in *Star Trek* terminology, with Gene Roddenberry. "First contact" refers to the initial encounter of the *Enterprise* crew with an alien species. A portentous event in any relationship, first contact is the fork in the road, the turning point, the open gate. From the televisions of the nation and the world, where *Star Trek* has been seen in one form or another for over twenty-five years, to the University of California Press series on the American genius, the phenomenon of Star Trek was creeping back slowly to its embryonic origin, its primal cell; contracting, like a star pulled together by gravity,[1] into its one intense point of creation, the mind of Gene Roddenberry.

I was early, an alien in a now familiar world. It seemed somehow appropriate as I approached the Hart Building that there were two skies at Paramount: the real one, brown and hazy, and the bright pristine "on a clear day you can see forever" one, standing on the lot like a giant drive-in movie, to make life on screen look real, or maybe to look as unreal as our perception of it.

We met before we met, in the manner of children—curious, apprehensive, and eager. For when I peered around the edge of the door that separated us, leaning to the left just enough to catch a glimpse of the man before we were introduced, there he was, leaning to the right, peeking around the door frame, just enough to catch a glimpse of me. In a kind of species recognition salute, we raised our hands and smiled, unstartled and, it seemed, mutually relieved. Someone introduced us, or didn't. My poster of Einstein was on his wall. The sun was shining—or wasn't. We looked at each other for a long time. This was our first conversation:

Me: You're not shy, are you? You look shy.

Gene: I think I can be.

Me: Oh dear.

Gene: Are you?

Me: No.

Gene: Okay. I won't be either.

.   •   .

The second time we meet, he says, "You haven't asked me one fact about myself."

"Do you want me to?" I ask.

"No. Not at all. Let's just talk, as we are."

I begin to launch into another subject.

"But why haven't you?" he interrupts.

I start to remind him that this isn't a biography, but he knows that. He wants the real answer.

The Conversation

"I don't think you are facts," I say. He looks at me with a
pleased, surprised wonder. "There is a passage in *The Little Prince,* which I read as a child," I tell him. "It made sense then. It continues to make sense." I quote the paragraph as accurately as I can:

> Grown-ups love figures. When you tell them you have made a new friend, they never ask you any questions about essential matters. They never say to you, "What does his voice sound like? What games does he love best? Does he collect butterflies?" Instead, they demand: "How old is he? How many brothers has he? How much does he weigh? How much money does his father make?" Only from these figures do they think they have learned anything about him.

Delight spreads across his face. "I think I am going to love telling you things," he says.

.   •   .

His voice sounded like tomorrow.
The game he loved best was being.
He collected ideas.

.   •   .

He sits back with some satisfaction. "Now," he says, "Let's see if we can figure out who this Gene Roddenberry is."

"Okay. What is the difference between truth and integrity?" I ask.

"Truth and integrity . . ." he muses. "Boy, you really cut through the crap, don't you?"

"I try." I pick up a copy of the *Humanist,* which features an extensive interview of him. "I was extremely impressed by something you said in here about relative truth. I think you said your fourth-grade teacher accused you of something you didn't do. And you defended yourself up to a point, and then just said, what the hell—yeah, I did it."

"Yes," he laughs.

"Well, some people will stand and fight forever and consider themselves people of integrity for having done so. Whereas you basically told a lie. If you know something to be true and it is true, and you try to explain it to someone who is not ready for it or doesn't want to hear it, do you undo yourself as a vehicle for true communication if you insist on facts as truth? Is that it? Are you offering a false image of yourself to insist on the truth—in these circumstances, I mean?"

"Oh yes, and there's so much of that. There are certain things you know to be true, the revealment of which is just not worth it—for all the losses you take. You have to be true to yourself. Let's explore that later, because that's typical of what I have done."

. • .

"Okay. What is the relationship between power and creativity?"

"Well, certainly they are related. I have a power in Star Trek that allows me to express my creativity, which I didn't have before. I think that relationship has something to do with the power of a free mind. A kind of freedom you feel inside yourself. I don't create if I don't *feel* my own power to do so. But really—I don't have a feeling of powerlessness. Generally, I do have a feeling of power."

The Conversation

Without freedom of choice, there is no creativity. Without creativity, there is no life.

"RETURN OF THE ARCHONS," *STAR TREK* (THE ORIGINAL SERIES)

· ● ·

"Do you know where it comes from?"

"I like to believe that it comes from the rich mix of things that—" he begins, then stops abruptly. He looks at me hesitantly. We do not know each other well enough yet. "No. I don't. But it's there. I've never doubted that my power was there. But I've had reason to doubt that I could force the world into marching the way I wanted it to march."

Until *Star Trek*? I wonder, but don't ask. I am assuming it will become clear.

"Who never fails you?"

"There's no person that has never failed me, any more than I am capable of not failing anybody. Humanity never fails me. They never fail me. But people? Oh yes."

"They?"

"Well, yes. I'm not speaking of my humanity, you see, but humans—all humans. Not individuals, but the whole human race. I think that humans are incredible. They are the most fascinating things in the universe."

"Well, but Gene, you haven't been through the whole universe. It may be that 'there are more things in heaven and earth, Horatio . . .' "

The Conversation

"There very well may be. That's what I try to show on *Star Trek.*"

"I want you to talk about that later. But first, tell me what the difference is between people and humanity."

"I have a theory about that. I call it a socio-organism. You see, the usual way of the physical world is to progress towards unity. When life originated on this planet, it was a single-cell organism. And perhaps by accident, or a need for survival, or some primal urge, these individual cells began to group together to form collectives, then units, then a corporate body. And that's what happens on a larger scale with humans. They form groups—tribes, nations, and so on. Even a simple working unit, like a business or a factory, is a socio-organism, because the individual units—or people—come together for a single purpose. Right now, in most cases at least, the purpose of collectives in society is functional: to produce a product, or to band together for economic or defense reasons. But if you follow the thought logically, you can project a more complex interaction—perhaps a thinking body in which the individual units no longer function in any capacity as individuals. They may specialize, but not without the knowledge and cooperation of the whole group. It's a kind of interdependence in which the whole is greater than the sum of its parts. I think this will form a new species, a human collective. I think we may be headed that way. It seems to me a natural consequence of evolution."

"Like the Gaia principle?"

"Yes, very much like that."

"Which means that it could be a step backwards if, as some scientists point out, we began that way."

"I don't think it is, though. It may be a recurring cycle, but it is a spiral. Each time we come around again, we will have learned something from our previous forms of unity. We may develop our capacity to . . . to think to each other, for example, to a higher level, each time we take another step in the evolutionary chain."

"Thinking to each other exists now, on a rudimentary level. You know people, don't you, that you would describe as being on the same wavelength—to whom you can give a quick glance to impart a thought?"

"Yes, I do. And I try to do that with as many people as I can. It rarely works," he says rather wistfully, then brightens. "But sometimes I am fortunate in that attempt. What I'm speaking of is large groups of people who have a group consciousness on a regular basis."

"Sounds like a convent or monastery to me."

"How would you know that?"

"Because I was in one, many years ago."

"What? You mean a convent school?"

"No. I mean a convent. You know: nuns, silence, uniformity, interdependence. Socio-organism."

He is dumbfounded. "You were a nun?"

"Yes. Don't worry, it's not contagious. But it is a socio-organism. We got to the point, living together day in and day out, largely in silence, that other forms of communication developed. It was fascinating. We could almost think to each other."

"When?"

"When what?"

"When were you a . . ."

"Nun. It's not a bad word. Nineteen sixty-six to sixty-nine. Same time as *Star Trek*. And, you know, that was one of the few programs that we were allowed to watch!"

He stares at me.

"It was a long time ago. A lot has happened since then. My point is that it was a perfect example of your socio-organism idea."

"Yes," he recovers. "Uh, how?"

"Mostly by regarding the face, rather than the dots. I was reading a book by Paul Davies, *God and Physics,* in which he discusses reductionism and holism. And he says that no amount of scrutinizing the dots on a newspaper picture can give you an adequate concept of what the face looks like. Whereas in a convent—or at least the kind I was in—the object is continually to form a face. Like on a starship, I suppose. Is that why you study humanity instead of people? To see its face? Why you look at the socio-organism as being representative of the true nature of man (humankind), rather than individuals?"

"I suppose it is. That is why diversity is so important. Because in diversity you can trace certain properties of the human spirit which transcend differences. It is only when you look at what unites humans, rather than what divides them, that you have some idea of what it means to be human."

"That's another thing Davies points out: that you can't always take a problem apart in order to solve it. Sometimes you only solve it by putting it together. And so you think that the human race is gradually moving towards an understanding of itself by creating a socio-organism?"

"I think that might be the case, although the argument for the individual is very strong. My socio-organism theory is that a certain individualism might remain, but become more and more specialized, so that one unit is proficient in one area, and another in another area. They are co-dependent, or really interdependent with all the others. So that the whole species becomes a true organism."

The Conversation

"Isn't that self-defeating?" I ask him. "Because who is left, then, to see the whole picture?"

"Yes, you have a point. It does tend to imply that the individual self, as we know it—as we conceive of selfhood—would be defeated. But that might not necessarily be a bad thing. Because maybe everyone sees the whole picture—there is a collective eye, so to speak."

"But how would we learn anything if we kept to our individual tasks? It sounds a bleak future, the antithesis of what your philosophy seems to offer."

"You did not feel it bleak in your convent, I'm guessing."

"No, not at all. But that was because the socio-organism of it was just that: socio. Or perhaps religio. It wasn't a single intellect organism. Each of us studied a variety of things, worked at an enormous number of tasks."

"Well, I haven't worked it out yet," he says comfortably, as though he were contemplating no more than his next move in a chess game. "What may function today as an organism or prototype organism may be very different from what we see tomorrow. And maybe there will be the opportunity for both individuals and cells in the great cosmic wheel. It just seems to me that it already exists—is somehow intrinsic to the need of humans to merge—and the impossibility of that being satisfied by individual mergings and couplings, such as marriages, or fragmented political or national entities—or religions. I feel that we are on the path to a collective that I can't quite visualize."

"But maybe you're looking at a metaphysical thing physically."

"What do you mean? I don't think I am."

"Well, let's consider you as the primal cell—your mind as an analogy of the first single-celled organism. That mind produces an idea like Star Trek, and within months the idea is transplanted into thousands, millions of minds as a modus operandi. These millions continue to do what they do, but in a way that speaks of and to the primal cell. Physically, socially distinct, but mentally, philosophically connected."

"Yes, for now," he says slowly, with an uncertain emphasis on "now," as though he is not quite sure what the word means. "But what happens as a result of that idea transplant is what I'm trying to see. This is just a stage. People want to do things with these ideas, and they will. And that draws them into contact with each other. And they build the kind of world in which perhaps a certain kind of diversity becomes extinct. That's what I worry about."

"Why? Diversity for its own sake isn't particularly helpful. It's one thing to celebrate it because it exists. It's another thing to mourn its passing if it no longer works. That's like saying people shouldn't marry other races because we have to preserve racial purity—that we have to stay distinct, diverse. The opposite of taking delight in diversity isn't to condemn it—it's just to allow it to change naturally. We may become diverse in ways we don't know about yet."

"Yes, that is true," he replies. "But that isn't what we can concentrate on . . . now. That's an idea for the future, when diversity has been celebrated and accepted. You're leaping ahead. And I suppose I am too, with my socio-organism idea. We mustn't do that. Humans are a fearful species. And I have certain fears about that too. But I have written a great deal about this, and I can give you my ideas on paper. Then we can discuss its moral implications.[2] I'd like to do that." He pauses and looks at me speculatively. "A *nun,* huh?"

"Yeah."

He shakes his head.

In a 1985 letter to his friend Dr. Charles Musès, Gene wrote: "Assuming the socio-organisms do continue to evolve more and more control of their human cells, successive generations of children will have less and less ability to act as individuals. Some interesting questions in this. Will the sorgs (socio-organisms) eventually win and destroy human individualism? Or is it possible the human creature is dividing (as some species in the past have done) and becoming two human types, individuals and sorg. No less interesting is the question of whether there are not pleasures and comfort in being a sorg cell that amply repay what is lost in giving up individualism? I don't know and maybe can't know because I'm so prejudiced in favor of individualism. . . . Agree that there is nothing intrinsically ethical about the size of human organizations per se, but somehow the citizens of the large developing nations with advanced education and media and medicine and technology do seem more civilized and peaceful than those of agricultural and pre-industrial nations. Could this suggest that the evolving of individual and sorg cells may be the pathway by which the cosmos' intelligent individual life forms into even more intelligent superorganisms? It pains me even to suspect this could be true— that is, it pains me until I require myself to think of it as an uncommitted intelligence (or scientist) might think of it."

· • ·

In *Star Trek: The Next Generation,* there is a race of half-humanoid–half-machine creatures called the Borg. The parallel with the sorg is striking, and yet the cybernetic Borg present a serious threat to the Federation. The original concept for the Borg was an insect race, and traces of that idea remain. Their collective mentality, homing instinct, and singleness of purpose are strongly reminiscent of the hive, or the anthill. Certainly, they are not the independent, spirited explorers of space one would expect to encounter in a race as technologically advanced as they. The Borg seem to have no spirit. They are devoid of feeling, devoid even of thinking. It is characteristic of the diversity of the Star Trek universe to include a rock creature who is a tender mother (the Horta in "Devil in the Dark," *Star Trek*, the original series) and a group of altered humanoids (Borg) who maintain their babies in filing cabinets ("Q Who," *Star Trek: The Next Generation*). In the years that preceded our discussion, Gene fluctuated between the fascination of collective consciousness and a fierce, fatherly protectionism for the independent individual of the human species. In keeping with a fine regard for the independence of the individual, he came down rather heavily in public in favor of individualism, hence the sinister threat of the Borg race. Privately, he didn't think it mattered all that much. He had thought about it a great deal, he told me, and if there were some cosmic insistence on unification, he believed it would take place as naturally and painlessly slowly as previous evolution. Whatever lifeform resulted would no more bemoan a previous state than we would now complain that we were no longer single-celled protoplasmic entities floating independently in a primordial swamp.[3]

· • ·

Nothing stares us in the face as we take our places at the table. It is a menacing sight, nothing. With its cavernous

hunger, without even the promise of a black hole—into
which one might metaphysically fall and contract, and
become a dense world among worlds—it seeks us from
across the table. The waiter brings bread. We are avoiding
fear. "What do you most fear?" I had asked him, not ten
minutes before, while the phones rang in his office, and a
secretary bobbed in and out on a wave of words like an er-
rant buoy. "Let's get out of here," he had said. Walking to
lunch, he answers the question. "Nothing," he says. And
now, in the commissary at Paramount Pictures, we sit
thoughtfully, crumbling bits of bread. Nothing grins mali-
ciously. Self-revelation is near. "Fear," Gene says, in a neutral
tone. "I wonder what else you're going to ask me." I hand
him my list of questions. He looks them over and decides to
be recalcitrant. "I think your questions are a lot more intelligent than my answers are going to be. I don't know if I can
answer them." Whoopi Goldberg, dressed as Guinan, walks
by.

"I don't see that 'What do you most fear?' is a particularly
brilliant question. And anyway, I'm not here to make you
look bad, as if that were remotely possible. Do you want to
avoid this question?"

"Yes, I do," he says. "But now that it's been asked, I don't
think I can. It's sitting here between us. The uninvited
guest."

"Oh, we invited him," I say. A waiter comes to take our
order. He is deferential, beyond the job requirement of serv-
ing egos and appetites. It is clear that Gene is warmly, personally, genuinely liked. Little things begin to appear on the
table, unasked for, and far more welcome than the unanswered question between us. Lemons and sugar, ice cubes
and wine, cream, extra cream, new flowers. Gene orders two

The Conversation

salads, and looks at me through narrowed eyes. He is not sure how I will take being ordered for. "It's a good salad," he says as though it were a challenge. "It's the best."

I thank him. Someone stops at the table. Gene introduces me. "This is my mistress," he says pleasantly. He lets the joke stand for a few minutes, waiting to see if I will correct it. I outwait him. He reintroduces me properly, and we chat for a few minutes. I see the possibility of discussing nothing fade. Later I find out that we have been speaking with a producer whose movies are household names. When a second person drops by the table, Gene introduces him to me as his lover. Nothing disappears.

"Humor as defense," I think, as I fly back to the Bay Area that afternoon with the question still unanswered. At 11:00 p.m. the telephone rings. "This is Gene Roddenberry," a now familiar voice announces. "I would like to answer that question." I get my notebook, which proves to be unnecessary. The answer is "Humanity."

I write in my notebook anyway, what he says next. "I have a great fear that our human leaders will fail to understand that a world such as *Star Trek* is possible, that all the glorious things—not that *Star Trek* represents, but that the human being represents—will fall on deaf ears. That frightens me. There's always a chance that not enough humans will understand and appreciate themselves enough to make a great change in the human equation."

It sounds like a prepared statement—unmistakably sincere, deeply motivated, but prepared all the same. I thank him for answering the question. He asks when I can come down next, reminds me that I will be staying at his house. We make a tentative arrangement. Just before we hang up, he asks, "What are you afraid of?"

The Conversation

I say I will write it down and give it to him when I get there.

"Oh good," he says. "I wrote mine down."

·   •   ·

Fear follows us into his office, one peculiarly clear morning. He wants to hear what I have written. I read it aloud:

I am afraid that evil will win out over good. I am afraid that there is no real wonder left in the world, which is why we as a species frantically try to create it—hence, Hollywood. I am afraid that I won't learn what I am supposed to learn before I die, and that it will somehow be my fault for not having tried hard enough. I am afraid that I will never touch the true human condition, because I've been too happy, and too fulfilled, and that, consequently, I am less human than I should be. I'm afraid of madness—not mine, but the fact that it exists—that so much can go wrong with the human brain. I'm not afraid to make the mistakes we all make (although I don't like to, of course), but rather, I am afraid that I might make the larger cosmic mistakes of missed destiny and dimensions unperceived. I'm afraid that I won't be able to do enough in my allotted span. And, I am afraid of surrender—not human connection, not intimacy—but surrender. Afraid of the power I have, because it is so difficult to translate into action accurately. I am afraid of pain for my children, my family. I'm not personally afraid of emotional pain—I don't seem to be vulnerable to that on the deepest level, but even that raises the question about whether or not that's a good thing. It may mean that I am not human enough. Afraid that the great cosmic truth, whatever it is, may be beyond my capacity to understand, if ever the time comes for me to understand it, and, therefore, I will be disqualified from vowing allegiance to it.

The Conversation

"Read it again," is all he says when I have finished. I do. I add that I do not necessarily believe these things—such as the fact that there may be no wonder in the world. I believe there is. But when worries do arise, they wear the garments of these concerns.

"I could have written that," he says. "Most of it. In fact, I'm not sure I didn't, somewhere in my mind." He frowns. "So, we share certain fears . . . who would have thought it?"

"Don't you want to add anything? Delete anything?"

"No. Nor do I want to discuss anything. Let it stand for the purposes of this book. It's enough for folks to think about without getting into detail." He looks at me keenly.

"What about nothing?" I ask him.

"Nothing?"

"You know, when I asked you last week what you were afraid of and you said, 'Nothing.' Was it a literal answer? Are you afraid of there being nothing out there, in the universe—that we may discover nothing? No creator? No cosmic consciousness? Nothingness?"

"I don't know. What would you say if I asked you the same question?" he replies, making circles on his finger with his thumb.

"I would say no. No, that's one thing I am definitely not afraid of."

"May I share that answer with you, until one of us knows for certain?"

"You don't want to discuss it."

"No."

. • .

He is afraid of that, of course. His particular mark of genius being the examination of all possibilities, he won't have
missed that one. But being afraid of a possibility does not
mean that one believes the possibility is probable. Or the reverse. He just doesn't want to talk about it. Yet.

I write a note to myself during this conversation: " 'The
Changeling,' original series—*Star Trek: The Motion Picture.*"
There are a few later scribbles in the margin, added as an
afterthought. One is a question from the Baltimore Catechism: "Who made you—and why?"

. • .

In one of Gene's films, *The Questor Tapes,* the protagonist,
Questor, is an android seeking his maker. His human friend,
Jim, accompanies him on a journey halfway around the world
to find the scientist who created him. At one point, when the
search seems futile, Jim says to Questor, "Suppose he isn't a
good man? Suppose he isn't even sane?" To which the android replies, "One's creator not sane? An interesting question. How would you answer that in your own case, my
friend?"

. • .

"The human race thus finds itself unique in the dubious
distinction of being the first biological species able—if it
continues on certain psychological collision courses—to
become insane. Fortunately, the diagnosis also indicates the
remedy," wrote Dr. Charles Musès, in *Destiny and Control in
Human Systems.* To which his old, dear friend Gene Rodden-

berry suggested that he include a passage from Christopher Fry's *A Sleep of Prisoners* to intimate the remedy:

> The frozen misery
> Of centuries breaks, cracks, begins to move;
> The thunder is the thunder of the floes.
> The thaw, the flood, the upstart spring,
> Thank God our time is *now,* when wrong
> Comes up to face us everywhere,
> Never to leave us til we take
> The longest stride of soul men ever took.

I ask Dr. Musès one dark December afternoon why Gene chose that particular poem. "It was a favorite of his," the great scholar replies. "It expresses his true religion—a far cry from atheism."

There is something dark and Decemberish in both of these minds: Both see illusion and reality exchanging places in an evolution to which they feel similarly responsible to bring some kind of light. There is, in fact, illumination between them. Gene Roddenberry called Charles Musès his mentor—refers to him now as a *most* intimate friend. He is the one person, Gene says, "who understood Star Trek long before I or anyone else . . ." There are secrets between them. There is mysticism.

· • ·

"What moves you?" I am prompted to ask, one day, watching the wind lift his hair. We are on our way to another lunch at the commissary. "Not moves as motivation, but what touches you, affects you?"

The Conversation

"I would say, it has to be the same answer: humanity."

I begin to feel that my book will consist of one word. "Gene," I say, "you're going to be terribly devastated if we do go out into space and find other lifeforms who are more fascinating than we are."

"Not 'if'—'when.' Space is humanity's future. And I don't know that that is necessarily true—they may be equally fascinating, not more."

"You don't think that there is a possibility that we may discover something more interesting than ourselves?"

"Oh, there's a good possibility," he says affably, in the reserved way that one mother acknowledges the beauty of another's baby. "But I haven't found it."

"Are you looking?"

"So far I have found nothing that says that humans are not supremely fascinating, supremely successful in the broad definition of what successful is."

.   •   .

"What moved him?" I can absolutely answer that for Gene. People. Humanity moved Gene.

ROBERT H. JUSTMAN

.   •   .

He was his own common denominator—as obsessive about humanity as though, from some cosmic coupling, he had spawned the whole human race. Every answer to every question, when reduced to its final sum, its primal end and beginning, was nothing less than all that we are: alpha, omega, and all in between. Humanity moved him, seduced him, terrified him—calmed, soothed, overjoyed, and perplexed him. It weighed him down, buoyed him up, inspired, and eluded him. In this preoccupation, he resembled nothing so much as Q.[4]

. ● .

When I ask Gene if he has a Q streak, he laughs and says yes. "Out of the mouth of Q come some very important Gene Roddenberry questions," he says. "We need to look at ourselves, examine who we are and why we are taking this fork in the road and not that one. Q has little or no compassion for the human race he loves to taunt, but that doesn't matter. It is the questions that matter. And how the human race will answer some of these questions for itself that ultimately will matter."

"What kinds of questions?" I ask him.

"Well, let me see, what is Q's challenge to the human race? To see the large picture, perhaps. To realize that there is a universe out there of which we are only a very small part. That we have more than a personal, a national, or even a global responsibility to evolve into a greater lifeform than we are. To find a broader definition for the word 'human' than we are currently comfortable with. And I think Q is there to show us the morality of power. You asked me about power and creativity. The correct use of power feeds creativity. And the misuse of power destroys it. Our people are very cautious of power in *Star Trek*—and rightly so. They are not ready for it. The human brain is still far too divided in its impulses to be reliable. But we are getting there. We are so much im-

proved in the twenty-fourth century. That is the beauty of
humanity. It continues to improve, despite its contradictory
impulses of creativity and destruction."

·　●　·

The next time he brings up a great love for humanity, I
ask him how he reconciles that with having killed people. He
does not mention his military service in World War II, but
instead starts to talk about a new series he has created in his
mind, which he will never make, about a society of subtle
and rational Hitlers. It is so terrifying that it answers the
question, but he goes on to say about the war that "those
things seemed necessary, and I seemed to be drawn into them
by necessity—perhaps by some ignorance." I ask him how a
twenty-fourth-century guy fights a twentieth-century war
and comes through unbroken. Suddenly, the air around us
changes. He recedes swiftly into a tunnel of time from which
he is normally free. He looks at me with my father's eyes,
from somewhere I have never been. I have seen that look a
thousand times in my lifetime, from a generation of men I
will never see again. "Don't ask," it says. "Stay ignorant. Stay
innocent. Be the daughters, wives, mothers we left behind.
Don't see what I am seeing. And please, don't understand."
He shakes his head unconsciously and I know that even now,
almost fifty years later, he will not answer my question. He
will give an answer, but not the one he would give to another
soldier, another guy. He returns from memory to philosophy,
and sighs.

"I'm not unbroken," he says, finally. "I'm patched up. And
it isn't because of a reason you might think of. It's not because of the violence and horror of war itself—although that

was terrible, really terrible. It's because it wasn't just some kind of mistake—it wasn't an aberration of man's nature. It *was* man's nature. It was because I came up against the manifestation of what had only been a fantasy for me—the existence, the persistence of evil. And something inside me broke when I found out that you can't fight evil with good, at least not always. You might be able to prevent it from erupting by being assiduously good, by making good choices, if enough people in a society make that choice. But after you've let it rise—and the people of Germany let it rise, and the world let it rise—you have to confront it with itself. You have to be what it is, in order to overcome it. You have to confront yourself."

"The enemy within?"[5]

"Exactly. That's what it means to know your enemy. And that's the real reason that we are both good and evil inside. So we recognize it in others—in movements and governments and so on. So we can survive."

"You mean two wrongs do make a right, after all?"

"Yes, sometimes they do. Two wrong actions—not two wrong motivations. If it was wrong for the Nazis to kill, it was just as wrong for us to kill. But it makes a difference what the reason is. And we have to live with that, and hope that whatever good comes out of it far, far outweighs the bad. And on the scale of human history, diplomacy is a recent invention. What we may once have fought over, we may now negotiate peaceably. But there is always so much ignorance and emotion to combat."

·   ●   ·

I do not object to violence itself, on television. I have a son growing up. There are some types of violence I would prefer for him to see. I

don't want him to see dishonest violence. I want him to see that if a
grown man hits another man in the face with his fist, that knuckles break, and bones shatter, and that is a messy, harmful, stupid thing to do. . . . If I had not been in a censored medium, the violence I would have shown on *Star Trek* at times would have been much more real. . . . We have had thirty-five years of war movies in this country, and usually the hero clutches his breast and dies very quietly, sometimes with a little smile on his face for having been able to give his all. I think during those thirty-five years, if our soldiers had died in pictorial depictions in movies and in television the way those of us who have been in combat know that men die, often screaming their guts out, we would have had a lot less people saying, yeah, let's send our kids to war.

CONGRESSIONAL STATEMENT OF GENE RODDENBERRY

.   •   .

For some reason, this reminds him of his days on the Los Angeles Police Force.

"About my being a policeman for a while . . . I never had any doubt that one of the great problems of modern times was how to force people to obey the law. It seemed to me at one time in my life that the best way to do that was to have policemen that were justifiable—policemen that were very *good*. Policemen who lived by what we consider the law. I think I would have done a better job than our current Chief Gates has done. At one time it was considered by some people that my natural future was to become chief of police."

"I'm glad you didn't."

He laughs, "I don't know . . ."

"Well there wouldn't have been any *Star Trek*."

"There wouldn't have been any *Star Trek*, but there would have been a much better police department."

The Conversation

"A Starfleet on earth? Yes, I'm sure you would have done an excellent job."

"I think I could have. And I had the courage to try new things. At one time I had decided that when I became chief of police, or when I graduated from being a police sergeant to police chief, I would bring along with me new attitudes and new uniforms, and that the only weapon you carried was one with which you could *choose* to injure or kill someone—or not. I felt there should have been shades of weaponry."

"Like phasers?"

"Like phasers."

"There is a kind of phaser out now."

"Yeah, tazers. And my thinking was innovative in many areas. I knew exactly the answer to the drug question. I had researched and written a piece for Chief Parker which pointed out that drugs created a no-win situation for the police. Unlike some police chiefs, I believed that we should legalize drugs—with penalties, with certain costs to their use, but in a way that it doesn't make a criminal out of you. I suspected that the answer to drugs did not lie in making them illegal. I would have done something like I have done in *Star Trek* for law enforcement. It might have failed, but that's the way I would have had it. I think it would have been a brave and bold try."

"Because people wouldn't be developing these highly toxic, instantly addictive drugs if they had access to other drugs, like in Switzerland? No reason to make cheaper street-value substances that do quick, irreparable damage?"

"Yes. And you wouldn't have had the underworld running America as they do today."

. • .

He tells me a little more about his Hitler series. It is about "a society of rational Hitlers," as he calls it, in which there is a far less visible erosion of fundamental precepts than history recounts. There is no suspicion, no opposition. Everything seems good. No one wakes up suddenly in horror, because everyone has given up the right to think, and therefore the ability to distinguish right from wrong. "We are creatures of *emotion,*" he says, "and what this said to humanity, during the time of Adolph Hitler, was that Hitler offered some things that we had relaxed our *thinking* about. And it would have gone Hitler's way, if he had been a rational man. I think that if Hitler had played his cards wiser, and better, and portrayed essentially the same person that he did—but with more care about what his real motives were—he would have won."

"You mean you think that people wanted what he had to offer?"

"Enough that he could have gotten by with it, yes, as long as he hid his true motives. People were passionately stupid about this need for a national emotion. To feel passionate about organization and order. To feel emotional about *things.*"

"Well, he was an irrational man. Irrationality often masquerades as high feeling."

"Thank God. Because if he had been a rational bad guy, he would have turned the world upside down. Oh yes, plenty of people wanted what he wanted—trains that run on time and all of the things that make life simpler. We were lucky in his irrationalism. And therein lies a beautiful series."

He looks at me piercingly. "Just think," he says intensely, "what would have happened if Hitler had been *good.*"

"Arthur C. Clarke wrote a novel, *Childhood's End,* which has some of that feeling."

"Yes, but the opposite happens in *Childhood's End.* The devils turn out to be decent guys."

"But the attitude of the people was similar. It looked like it was going to be a Hitler situation."

"Yes, it did. It was a great book, wasn't it?" he asks, glancing at the row of Heinleins, Asimovs, and Clarkes on his bookshelves.

"Yes. Compelling. But here's something I want to ask you. What difference would it have made, philosophically, if Hitler had been good but if he espoused the same premise—which I suppose was that he knew best, and would think act and operate on behalf of everyone—and used the same fervent oratory? You still end up with an unthinking populace. Or does goodness not permit autocracy?"

"Those are some of the questions that I am exploring in this series."

"Got any answers?"

"One. That good can be evil, and evil can be good, depending on circumstances. And that's a very good question you asked about, well, about ends and means. Of course, the atrocities that went on wouldn't have happened—and that is good. But as to your question about an unthinking populace—well, this is something that frightens me, as I told you. And yet, there are so many out there who don't know how to think, and *think* that they think. Well, I don't know. People need leaders. And I think it is absolutely imperative that they be good, decent people. But as to whether they should, in their goodness, allow others less qualified to participate in decisions that they are incapable of making, no—that isn't goodness, it's disaster. I wouldn't let anyone do that in my show. And I hope I'm basically a good man. But I know my show. *I* decide. You see, you get someone writing a marvel-

ous script, for example—really first-class. And they have a
thousand extras in it, and hundreds of thousands in special
effects. And it's filmed in Tokyo. And they keep saying, 'But
it's a good script, it's a good script.' Yes, it is, but I can't use it,
because I know what it takes to make a television show. Or
they have Picard getting drunk and shooting someone—in a
story that would be excellent for another show—a way of
demonstrating a heroic flaw. But it's not *Star Trek*. It's not
Picard. He wouldn't do that. This is the twenty-fourth century, and Picard is Picard, with his own flaws—which I created. And, of course, I won't use it because it's not *Star Trek*.
And this kind of power that I have is not because I'm
smarter—no. In fact, put that same writer in my office for a
couple of days and he'd smarten up astronomically. My
power comes as the creator, and because *I know my work*. And
that's a rather silly example of the kinds of decisions I make
in my work. And I expect from our leaders in government,
science, medicine, commerce, the same kind of knowing. I
think we must insist on a kind of excellence of mind, of experience. And if that experience means age, then age, in our
leaders. I think we have to look for something that cannot be
measured or analyzed, but it can be recognized and that is
the quality of leadership itself. The ability to feel and think in
balance, the ability to engender emotion for rational aims.
Really, I sometimes wonder if it wouldn't be wise to have an
emotional president and a rational one. Equally in power."

·   •   ·

On October 13, 1992, a little more than a year after this
conversation, Jon Carroll, a columnist at the *San Francisco
Chronicle,* publishes a piece "We Really Need a New King

Thing." His complaint: "The American President is both head of the state and the head of government and that just ain't right. . . . The British have a Prime Minister and a Queen. Of course, we can't have a king," Carroll explains, "because we fought an entire war so that America would never be ruled by a king. So not a king, but a king thing. We need a name for the job, that's the first step. **We need a name that commands respect the world around,** and yet is free from old associations and connotations. Not proconsul, duke or chief. Not mogul, sultan or CEO. Not satrap or secretary or emperor. We need a name that is at once familiar and new. The new job should be called **Captainkirk.**"

This person, he goes on to say, should have "physical stamina, natural dignity, and an established place in the culture" and "the President and the Captainkirk would rule jointly. . . ."

It isn't a serious proposal, of course. But it could be. I wish Gene could have seen it.

.   •   .

"I think there are some who simply must be told what to do, by compassionate leaders," Gene continues, in this same conversation. "But told respectfully. You see, Captain Kirk is a good man. And he is also an excellent man—well trained, experienced. But he is a man who was *born* to be a leader. And whatever that is, it is what makes him capable of convincing others who are less experienced, less able, to allow him to lead. In his leadership, he gives others the opportunity to grow. He isn't so in love with leading that he forgets his duty. His duty is to seek out life—and that also means the lives in his care—to bring them along, to see that they have the opportunity to learn and grow to their fullest. Their fullest may not be a quarter of what Kirk's is, but it's theirs and they have a right to it."

"Are we talking about Kirk or Gene or Hitler or the president of the United States?"

"All leaders. That's why I have this series in my mind about leadership and power. It's a series that I'll never make, though. I don't think I want to get into another gigantic series."

"It does sound daunting. But then, you never get tired of *Star Trek.*"

"No. But if I wanted to fit my brain for this new series, I could find many reasons that I would like to show the Hitlers in this way—so there would be weeks passing by, without any sign that they were fucking the world. And we would see how people would respond to that, the conflict of emotion and freedom. The need to feel part of something and the coldness of rational freedom. But I'll never make it. I just don't feel like it right now."

"What do you feel like, right now?"

"Writing, I think. I have so many ideas in mind. Most of them are books. Some may survive the translation into television or film. I don't know. Right now, at the moment, I like being here with you, talking about the things that matter to me. Because they don't just matter to me, you see, they matter to everyone—even if they don't know it. It is a terrible mistake to think that the future is somewhere off in a distant time. It is here, in embryo. We are creating it right now, with the decisions we make about the environment, with the attitude we take towards space exploration, with the education we are giving our children. Everything." He sighs and shrugs his shoulders, like Atlas shifting the earth to a more comfortable position. "But, talk to me for a little while. Tell me what comes into your mind because of what I have said."

"A lot of things. Most of all, the way we think, the way we struggle with our thoughts and never let them free. Just freeing a thought sometimes makes enormous changes. Saying, "I wonder if there could be some way to have light without fire"—and that leads to electricity. I love the way you dreamthink. And I think that dreamthink is what makes *Star Trek* what it is, neither an appeal to the emotions nor an argument for cold rationalism. It's both, and therefore neither. And that gives credence to prescience—to all the inventions and attitudes, all the thoughts and habits and cultures, diversity we encounter in *Star Trek*—and the diversity that I am beginning to find in you. It brings time into perspective. It changes the meaning of tomorrow. When you say 'education'—it's not just a word that means a passport to a linear series of events in an individual's life. It means the education of the species."

"Oh," he says animatedly. "I've given so many lectures on that very concept. And people are so frightened of it; they never comment on it. They pretend they didn't hear that part of the lecture. Or if they mention it, they say, 'Yeah, neat, great idea.' But they are terrified."

"Terrified about what?"

"The giving up of cherished concepts. Things they think they need to be able to recognize themselves as human beings."

"Like what?"

"Like anything. Think of something fundamental to your beliefs that you wouldn't be willing to give up."

"Give up in favor of what?"

"Well, now," he says, raising both hands in a kind of universal appeal, "you see, that's a question that most people just don't get around to asking. They think of something dear to them and panic—won't go any farther in their thoughts."

"Oh, well, that doesn't make any sense to me. Thoughts are the only province of pure being left to us. Besides you don't have to do anything about what you think. You can just think it. And anyway, I do have some experience in at least the metaphysical sacrificial aspects of life. I gave up just about everything when I went into the convent."

"Except your beliefs."

"Oh no, no, not at all. I had no beliefs when I went in that I wasn't willing to give up. And I had no beliefs when I came out that I wasn't willing to give up, for a good reason. Don't mistake Catholicism for a religion. It isn't. It's a nationality, as someone once said. Belief has very little to do with it."

"How could it not?" Gene asks. He seems to be having a very good time asking questions. We will have an argument later about this very fact. He will win.

"It really isn't necessary to believe like a Catholic," I tell him. "It's only necessary to think like one. Because, in the end, after all that study and training and a lot of things that you can't possibly know, and I'm not going to tell you right now, what I found out was that the only requisite belief—for those who explore it deeply enough—is the supremacy of 'an informed conscience.' That's what they tell you in the end—and what the Jesuits sometimes, and the Benedictines usually, hint at in theology classes, like you hint around at things in *Star Trek* and hope that people will recognize. The rest of the stuff is for the people who don't. And what that means is self-governance—'mortifying the passions' and all that—for those who choose it. And blind obedience for those who don't. Like Star Trek."

He looks very surprised, and very interested. "Like Star Trek. Hmmm. Well, but what does it mean to think like a Catholic?"

"Gene, I am supposed to be interviewing you."

"Well, it is *I* who wants to know."

"Okay," I shrug. I figure that I can just eliminate this conversation when it is time to put the book together. "Well, briefly it means a habit of rational analysis, no matter how irrational the premise, a constant awareness of culpability, an internal detachment from all but primary exigency. It means a large vocabulary at a very young age, which includes words and phrases like 'transubstantiation' and the difference between actual grace and sanctifying grace. And, oh, Gene, it's a whole culture. It means being able to explain those things to the satisfaction of a series of philosophically exacting instructors; it means a grounding in Latin that results in making English words mean to oneself something other than their colloquial use would generally imply; it means carrying around a world of images—and thinking in metaphors—living in a metaphorical world. Nothing is really literal after you've finished the two thousand questions or so in the Baltimore Catechism at age seven. It all seems to apply to everything except the dogma, which one soon learns is another metaphor—made literal for the lazy or the inept. Or at least that's the way it was and, I suppose, remains for many people my age. I don't know—I haven't been involved in that in years. The point is, it's just another Star Trek, if you separate the content from the form, and deal with . . . well . . . with what *is*."

I can see his mind buzzing, but we are not yet quite known to one another. He is being careful. He says only, "But I wonder if most people separate things like you and

I. I don't think so somehow. It's something I am still trying to find out. I think, so far, that they are afraid of detachment. Of being detached from what they perceive as themselves. Which is why I think my socio-organism idea would work. And anyway, I may have been a little cruel in my insistence on the giving up of cherished ideas. I don't remember. I just remember that I scared quite a few people."

· • ·

Unclouded vision ahead requires that you deal with *what is*. To deal with *what is,* you must free your forebrain of your personal value system and personal preferences. You must discard all, or at least most, of your prejudices. Not just simple intolerance about race, religion, and so on. It is much more difficult than that. You must free your mind of those values dearest of all to you: affection for your home, your background, your country, its customs, your own culture, your religious beliefs. The more precious the belief to you, the more certainly it must go if you are to free your forebrain to use its perception and logic. Some very able and intelligent people are unable to endure this exercise, even for a few hours. Some people get angry at even the suggestion that they drop all their preferences. Almost a castration complex—"I can't give that up!"

At a recent conference, someone asked: "Why go to all that trouble? Why not just read some good books about the future?" Which falls into the category of questions you wish that pleasant, intelligent-looking people didn't ask. Aside from the not inconsiderable advantages of learning to *free* your forebrain to do what it is clearly designed to do, I shudder at the thought of anyone making a trip as important and perilous as tomorrow while depending totally on someone else's vision.

GENE RODDENBERRY, UNIVERSITY LECTURE, 1983

The Conversation

"Well, anyway, tell me, give up in favor of what?"

"I certainly don't need to answer that question for you. And I'm not going to answer it, personally, for publication. I'll tell you later. But perhaps I will say this for publication: In favor of not letting the concerns of our animal brain override the impulses of our forebrain. To somehow distinguish between intelligence and instinct."

· • ·

We know now that each of us has an early brain combination, which we can call our "animal brain," which supplies our unthinking needs such as heartbeat, reflexes, and other body operations necessary to life. It also provides us with our emotions, fear, anger, hunger, lust, family protection—all the drives we've needed in order to survive and to reproduce.

That animal brain is relatively small and simple compared to the wondrous thing that rises out atop it. Wow! If you want to feel awed and humble at whatever created us, you need only consider our magnificent forebrain, the cerebrum. That forebrain, too seldom described even to us who own them, is a mini-micro-miniaturized wonder that makes our finest computers look in comparison like simple baby-blocks.

Let me now cup that forebrain within my palms here. And I invite those who want to share a very unusual feeling to do the same. Try it. You might like the feeling. Incidentally, despite whatever you might have heard, all of us have almost identical-sized brains.

Ready? We are holding within our palms now ten billion electrical signal-producing neuron cells . . . with each of those ten billion neuron cells able to interact in different patterns with as many as twenty thousand other neuron cells. Which means . . . that this "natural computer" small enough to fit within our palms, is capable of three hundred trillion interconnections, which gives this young and frail human creature's mind an options potential equal to the total number of stars in our galaxy!!! . . .

Our magnificent forebrain does all those things which make us "human." It gives us our ability to think consciously, to love, to write poetry and great symphonies, to theorize about relativity, to study quasars millions of light years away and, at the same time, look deep inside the construction of the atom, and of our gene cells too. It also gives us reason, with which to regulate our smaller, sometimes too selfish but very necessary animal brain.

Our "animal within us" brain is lovely in its way, too. Its insistent, basic message: Survive! Reproduce! is not the "evil" part of us—unless nature and life are evil things. In fact, the animal brain is capable of simple and marvelous delights—that part of ourselves which propels us into dance, and into song, and into sacrificing for our families.

Why can't we control that simpler brain? Well, the fact is that we do control it! Billions of humans succeed in doing that every day. Very ordinary people like us have controlled it even in the face of torture and death.

Dare we learn more about how to control it? **Dare we not learn that?** There is something patently obscene about a three-hundred-trillion-options magnificence being held hostage by a small, simpler, half-tamed animal thing.

GENE RODDENBERRY, UNIVERSITY LECTURE, 1983

.   •   .

"What about the reverse?" I ask him. "Allowing instinct to take over sometimes? I mean, the ability to do something: The intelligence needed to create a nuclear weapon, for example, is at variance with the instinct to survive, and logic dictates some sort of 'discard mechanism'—an idea

The Conversation

dumpster—in the animal brain which would rule in favor of survival."

"That is an interesting way of looking at it—backwards, yes. But I think that recognizing the implications of an intelligent act, such as creating the bomb, would also rest with the forebrain. The forebrain then informs the animal brain that it is dangerous, and then instinct takes over."

"So the object may be to create a third mechanism—the synthesis brain—which does not think sequentially, but operates outside time and sees all ramifications at once."

"That's called wisdom," he says. "And some humans already have it. But unfortunately not the ones who should. Not the ones with the power."

"You have quite a lot of power. Do you feel it an obligation to be wise?"

"I feel an obligation to try. I like that concept of spontaneous synthesis. That's what we have in computers today. And coupled with the human brain—we have the future, not only in our hands, but quite literally, in our minds. I think we are getting closer to the time in which computers will be part of our internal structure—as we have false joints and pacemakers and other wonderful things that enhance human life now. Computers are as close to an answer about the future as we'll ever have right now. When I laid out our first design for the Bridge, in the first series, I had only a general idea of what should be there. I knew that the quickest way to generate information was to have buttons that you pushed that would somehow connect to all that information in the computer. And without knowing what they were—what they meant—I just knew that they should be there. There was nowhere in those days where you could go to get a computer keyboard. We had to make ours out of wood! We *predated* the computer generation. That's why the computer industry was so helpful to us—back in the days when they were just solving certain mysteries, we were presenting and solving mysteries too. This is why they have been so supportive over the years. We kept having the experience of going to a top-rated computer company and having the boss say, 'Give them whatever they want!' It was grand to have them say, 'Take the shop. You *Star Trek* people obviously know more about it than we do!' We received hundreds of thousands of dollars' worth of information and help. And NASA too."

"I have a question," I say, wondering if I should ask it.

"You always do," he smiles. "And always ask it. There isn't anything that you can't ask me."

"Okay. It's about androids—which are the most sophisticated example of future computer technology currently under serious discussion—and the human brain. Would you like to be an android?"

"You have a reason for asking that question that I would like to hear before I answer it."

"Why? So you can tailor your answer? I don't want you to do that."

"No, so I can answer the question you are really asking. I'm not sure what it is."

"On *Star Trek*," I say, looking at him skeptically, "there are so many instances of mind transference, of telepathy, of entities cohabiting the same body, and of mechanical or computer interaction with humans or humanoids. 'The Lights of Zetar' creatures, the androids in 'I, Mudd,' Roger Korby in 'What Are Little Girls Made Of,' Kolos, in 'Is There in Truth No Beauty?' Landru, Sargon, the Controller in 'Spock's Brain'—and probably a lot more that I can't remember offhand. The Vulcan mind-meld has properties of mental intercommunication between beings, although generally it appears to be one-way: Spock reading the other person's thoughts, not the other way around. But it's the android thing that puzzles me."

"Yes, we did do a lot of shows like that," he says noncommittally. "What's on your mind?"

"In every instance that I've mentioned, except the mind-meld, those connections are portrayed as undesirable. Perhaps less so in 'Is There in Truth No Beauty?'—but even so, it is a threat. But there is something about it that doesn't quite . . . ring true."

"What makes you say that?"

"I don't know. Intuition, I guess. That, and also, those examples are all from the first series. When we get to the first movie—ten, twelve years later—you have Commander Decker disintegrating into a universe of molecules so that he can merge with V-ger, which is basically a computer even though you call it a 'living machine.' And this giving up of purely human life is portrayed with great excitement and anticipation—with exhilaration and celebration."[6]

"Yes."

"Then comes *Star Trek: The Next Generation,* and there are Trills, Bynars, Borgs, and even Data, who, although purely android, engenders some of the same questions about life, or 'livingness.' "[7]

"I think I know what you're going to ask. Why did I treat those two concepts so differently, between the original series and *The Next Generation?*"

"Not quite. My question is, in fact, did you? It seemed to me that in 'I, Mudd,' for instance, when Uhura says she would like to have her brain implanted in an android body, to give up a purely human existence, you cut and go to com-

mercial, and the audience is supposed to be horrified by
that—by her desertion of her allegiance to flesh and
blood—during those two minutes or so, until the next segment resumes."

"Well, the audience is supposed to be persuaded to buy
things from the sponsors in those two minutes, but I know
what you mean."

"Yeah, but I think *your* reason was to implant a moment of
consideration of that possibility—a subliminal flash that it
might just be something to think about. And then we come
back, and it turns out that it was just a ruse. Uhura was stall-
ing for time, and humanity triumphs once again. But does it?
I mean, what is wrong with an android body equipped with a
human brain? And isn't that an idea *you* stuck in *my* mind by
doing that show? And isn't that an example of conveying a
truth by telling a lie—because, really, you're showing something to be bad that you think might be good? In other
words, is it better to present the idea, in whatever light, than
not to present it at all? Or am I seeing things that aren't
there?"

"Which question do you want me to answer?"

"All of them."

"Well, the simple answer is, I think, yes to everything except the last question. You're seeing things that are there. But
I can't really give a simple answer, because I think that humanity is not ready to deal with the implications of all that
would mean. Morality plays a large part in these considerations. I think that discussing the morality of this currently
impossible technology for a century or so might bring us
closer to the responsible use of this technology when it does
become available. So, yes, I did intend that people think
about these things. And no, I did not intend that they should

now adopt the notion as a good one—only as a possible one, whose goodness or evil depended on its use."

. • .

Star Trek has always been a morality play. That's what it is about. That's what it's saying. You have all the premise you need to do a show like *Star Trek*—all you need to do is know the Ten Commandments. Morality is the subject that has intrigued humankind since the dawn of time. And will always continue to intrigue humans.

ROBERT H. JUSTMAN

. • .

"And what about the first question?"

"What was that?"

"Would you like to be an android? Or rather to have your brain transferred to an android body?"

"Well, I haven't been very well lately, so that presents an attractive option for me. I'd certainly consider it. And, as you say, in *The Next Generation* we are more comfortable with these things. Audiences have changed tremendously over that last twenty-five years. And, more importantly, for the show at least, I am as near to an absolute monarch as is possible in this industry. I have complete control over what my show says and does. Much, much more freedom. And far more direct responsibility for what goes out there to the audience. *I* am *Star Trek*. And as you say, we have wonderful options for interconnections between beings. I believe in those connections. I'm fascinated with the mind-meld, with the Bynars, with the Trills. To be able to understand another being, or beings, that intimately . . . oh yes."

The Conversation

"Would you choose to be half of an entity? I can't imagine that you would."

"No. But I might like to let someone share me for a while, or I might like to share someone. But as a permanent condition, no. But others might. I don't create these shows entirely for myself. I seek out what humanity yearns for."

"What do you yearn for?"

"I said you could ask me anything. I didn't say that I would be able to provide an answer. If I knew, I would tell you, because whatever it was, I think you would understand it. But I just don't know. What do you yearn for?"

I tell him.

"Oh," he says. "Maybe that's it. But I don't think that's something I want to say right now."

"The preceding announcement was brought to you by the public Gene Roddenberry," I tell him.

He smiles. "I *am* a public figure." He looks into my face for a moment. "Don't worry," he says. "They'll figure it out."

.   ●   .

Twenty-five months after his death, there will be an article in *Omni* magazine, "Souls in Silicon" by Frederick Pohl and Hans Moravec. Its subtitle is "Transferring the human brain to a computer may no longer be science fiction."

"The future *is*," I hear Gene saying as I begin reading, "not the future *will be*."

.   ●   .

We are having a particularly interesting breakfast. He is watching the news, I am reading a novel by Anita Brookner. We are both comfortable. That's the interesting part. When the news is over, he turns off the television and I put down my novel. We sit companionably for a few moments.

"I asked you once who never fails you," I say. "Now tell me what never fails you."

"My imagination never fails me. I don't leap spontaneously into an unfailing technique. I'm not that clever. I have to live with a thing in my mind for a considerable period of time—a character, for example. What never fails me is my optimism that in time I'll solve the problem that this thing poses. I can't promise myself that I'll do it rapidly, but sometimes I surprise myself. I have a rich mental life. That's why I had to make *Star Trek*. I felt I had something of importance to say, and if I could say it in a way that was entertaining to others, then maybe they would listen."

"What should they hear, when they listen?"

"Oh, so many, many things. What comes to mind right now is space. Space is so important, because it affects our whole future. There is no doubt that we are going into space. *Star Trek* offers us the opportunity to choose big hunks of the future. How will we go into space? What is necessary? And I don't mean technology. I mean the development of the person—of all people—what kind of beings do we want to be? What can we give, and how will we make ourselves capable of giving ourselves to the experience of the future?"

.   •   .

Mankind will reach maturity on the day it learns to value diversity—of life and ideas. To be different is not necessarily to be ugly; to have a different idea is not necessarily to be wrong. The worst thing that could happen is for all of us to look and think and act alike. For if we cannot learn to value the small variations among our own kind here on earth, then God help us when we get out into space and meet the variations that are almost certainly out there.

GENE RODDENBERRY

.   •   .

Further conversation reveals that Gene believes it is the philosophy inherent in *Star Trek* which offers the opportunity to "choose big hunks of the future." It means thinking of space as one's natural environment, of earth as one's temporary home, of country as one's school, and region as one's flavor. Family is everyone it can be, and love never means possession, greed, dependence, hobby, romance, sex, money, or revenge. Love in this world means *caritas,* an impersonal, impartial, universal regard for the sanctity of all lifeforms. Above all, to Gene it means a passionate existence within oneself, a deep connection with the variety of beings that we each are inside. His credo is Socratic: Know thyself.

"To whom do you always listen?" I ask him. "Or almost always. Nobody listens to anybody all of the time."

"Really, no one. I have no such person or group. I listen to the voice of, I listen to my inner logic."

"Where does it come from?"

"I don't know. It comes from—they come from—" he is changing his answer as he speaks. "This is a very weird thing. It's just an inner logic, an imagination that is right for me." Later he will contradict, expand, incorporate this statement into self-revelation. Later, when he is ready, he will tell me about Spock.

"But many people have a friend or brother or someone to

whom they will always pay attention when that other person speaks, because they trust their judgment on important issues."

"I have no such person. So I guess the answer to that is: me!"

"Yes, I guess it is."

"You know that proposes—that sets frightening goals for me: to know I know the answer. And I don't pretend that in every aspect of the world that I do know the answer. But I don't know anyone who knows it better than I do."

"So, you are self-contained. At least, you are if you consider your imagination to be you, or part of you."

"Yes, I am self-contained. But I'm not sure if my imagination is part of me, if anyone's is part of them."

"What would it be, if it wasn't?"

"A mystery. A flashlight in the dark. God."

"You're pretty well known for not believing in God. Do you claim him now?"

"Oh, well, people are often pretty well known for things which are not true."

"Well, is it?"

"No, it's not. I believe in a kind of god. It's just not other people's god. I reject religion. I accept the notion of God."

"But if you claim him as personal imagination or source of imagination, then he, she, it, is not just a notion. You're begging the question, distancing it. 'The notion of God' is not the same thing as God."

"No, but they are equally abstract. I don't humanify God."

"No. You just deify humanity."

He laughs. "Okay, look, whatever it is, we can't know it. But it very well may be there."

"Gene . . ."

"That answer doesn't satisfy you."

"Does it satisfy you?"

He frowns for a moment. "No, no, it doesn't. Let me think about it."

"I think you've thought about it. Perhaps you just don't want to reveal your thoughts. If so, just tell me."

"You're a hard person to dodge. And I don't want to dodge you, or the question. Yes, I have thought about it." He pauses. "Alright. God, to me, is intrinsic to humanity. To the whole cause of humanity. To the imaginative principle. To what we create, and think. He—or I should say 'it'—is a source, yes, but more an involvement with the unknown. God is like the leap outside oneself—something that has no discernible source, but is a source."

"Inspiration?"

"That's as good a word as any. Better than most."

"Well, the origin of the word is *inspiro,* from the Latin, meaning 'to breathe into.' Suggesting, in your definition, a breath of life from an unknown source."

"A breath of life. I like that. It is a breath of life, this god thing. It's not a thing you pray to, it's a thing you use to answer your own prayers. Humanity needs God in order to be humanity—it is part of them."

"Them. Not us."

"You've caught me again."

"Why 'them,' Gene? Are you not human?"

"Yes . . ." He sounds hesitant. "Yes. Yes. Of course I am."

"I'm not sure that's true."

"Oh, I am. At least, my body is. This vessel is." He shakes his head dismissively.

"Well, we'll go back to that one. What I'm trying to ascertain is if you believe in a spiritual life."

"What do you mean exactly?"

"Do you believe that there is an existence beyond empiricism, beyond the body, beyond the mind?"

"I don't know that one exists."

"I know you don't *know*. Nobody knows. *Credo quia absurdum.*"

"Translate, please."

"It means 'I believe *because* it *is* absurd.' In other words, one *believes* because one *can't* know. That is essentially the nature of belief. Faith—in anything—the existence of aliens—the ability to overcome obstacles—some form of God. It's not about knowing. It's about believing, in oneself or anything else."

"Yes. I have faith in something that I can't know, but I don't know what that is. It's not the traditional Judeo-Christian God. It's that thing about humanity that makes them write poetry, paint great pictures—"

"Create Star Trek."

"Oh, yes, that was a leap of faith. Creating Star Trek was a very spiritual experience, in that definition . . . It really is a life beyond this one," he adds, flipping into metaphysics. "It's my world."

"Let's go back to 'them.' You can't seem to stop referring to humanity as though it were a separate species from yours. Why do you do that?"

"I don't know. I really don't. But I feel . . . apart, sometimes. Perhaps that's why I try so hard to connect to people. To humanity. I think many writers, poets, artists, stand apart. They are essentially creators, and creators, as someone said, have a spark of divine fire. Or, as you said, a breath of life. Perhaps it's that divinity in us that we call God. The creative principle. Answer the question yourself. Do you feel part of humanity?"

"This book isn't about me."

"But I'm interested."

"Oh, I'll tell you, but it's not going to form part of this book, so I'll just turn the recorder off."

"No, don't do that. I'm not here to pontificate. This is a dialogue, a dialectic. I find myself saying the things I say only because of what you say and ask. It's marvelous. It really is very liberating. That piece you wrote on the things that frighten us—that's the sort of thing that brings something into view which I wouldn't perhaps do on my own."

"We still haven't talked about it," I reply, thinking that it is perhaps the fear of there being no existence outside existence that makes it so difficult to address these questions.

"No, but we will. I'm thinking about it. And it's unlikely that I would be thinking about it right now without that interchange."

"But, Gene—"

"No," he says stubbornly, "now don't try to dodge me. You bring out who I am and what I think by who you are, what you ask. I want you to record this conversation. I want this book to be a conversation."

"Gene, look, the purpose of this book is to portray who you are, not who I am. Nobody's going to care what I think."

"Then they would be very foolish. There is a wonderful thing created between two people of like minds when they communicate. What arises between us is some kind of truth. And it only arises because you are you and I am me. If people want to know who I am, through this book, then they have to look at who you are. Because I choose it. Because you, you discover me. I might not even know what I really think in some instances, until a door that I had forgotten—or didn't even know was there—opens between us. That's the wonderful thing about a conversation—if it's a real one, if it's

The Conversation

communication. It's like sex, which can result in a child. You have to have two parents if you want a child. This book between us is a child."

"Don't be silly. You could dictate your thoughts into a tape recorder."

"But they wouldn't be these thoughts. We're exploring Gene Roddenberry together. It's something that, at this stage of my life, is important to me. I want to continue to do that, as companions on an inner journey, as inner friends. I'm tired of interviews. This is a dialogue. It is creation. You can be, and are, that breath of life for me."

"So basically what you're saying is that I am God."

"Certainly. We both are. There is life here, isn't there?"

"Yes, but—"

"Then it's *our* book. And I can't reveal myself, for this purpose, without you. I really can't, you know. I'm not just saying that to be difficult. Besides, you can learn a lot about a person by the questions he asks of others. It shows what is in his own mind, what kind of quest he is on. I think what we're doing here is a marvelous example of what I'm trying to achieve—have always tried to achieve in *Star Trek*."

"Which is?"

"You tell me."

"To seek out new life—contact."

"Contact. Yes. Now please, answer my questions and I'll answer yours," he says. "Do you feel that you are part of humanity?"

It seems a strange question to ask, even though I have just asked it. But then, I do not refer to humanity as "they." There is something hovering in his mind he can't quite reach. Nor can I. Suddenly old catechetical distinctions leap into my mind: "One is responsible for creating one's own soul."

The Conversation

"Yes," I reply, "whenever I'm not creating something else."

"You see, you see, that's exactly what I mean. You've just sparked something I want to talk about: the creative process."

"Good. Talk."

"Well, you've said, 'whenever I'm not creating something else.' It's that 'something else' that intrigues me. Because, you see, there really is a something else, as you know, as I know. I don't know what it is, but I go there—it's a place, really—when I want to create something. I, I think it's imagination, but that doesn't explain it fully. I feel very alone, you know. And I'm happy in that. I love myself. But when I go there—to this place of creativity, to this area of the mind—I know that's where I belong. What I find there—whether or not they are characters or ideas, whether or not they are the product of my own mind—are the species I belong to. What happens is that I bring them out into this world, the world of humanity, and they take their place among them." He gives me a quick smile. "Among *us*. But I don't think I create them. They already exist. I just, I just introduce them. That's really where the whole idea of Star Trek came from—from that place, or state of mind. And the creative process is not so much in determining what or who they are, or what they look like; it's figuring out how they will get to where we are. That's my job. That's my contribution. They will reveal themselves, who they are in our world. I'm just a vehicle, a transporter."

"So you reach into a sort of cosmic Oz, and drag them back to Kansas."

"Yes. Although sometimes they come willingly."

"How?"

"I meditate. I think. I tune in, turn on, drop out, as Timothy

Leary says. Or said. I don't think he is saying that nowadays."

"Tune in, turn on, drop out of what?"

"Myself, first of all. That's the tuning in. Or actually, the dropping out comes first. I just refuse to be part of this world for the time I am thinking. Then, then I tune into myself—I discover myself. And that turns me on, in two ways. Literally, I become excited about myself, my own mind. There's so much in there. And I turn on a kind of mental screening room—you know the screening rooms over at the studio, it's like that. I watch whatever is on the screen. I watch their faces, their movements. I see their backgrounds. I listen to their voices."

"Sort of a 'burning at the stake' activity."

"In another century, yes. Thank God, humans have gotten beyond that stage." He thinks about this last statement, corrects himself: "Are getting beyond that stage."

"Why can't people get to Oz themselves? Or is that a question of Muhammad and the mountain?"

"People are afraid of that sort of thing. And I'm not a guru, dealing in states of Nirvana, for others. It takes a great deal of energy, a great deal of longing, to get into that cosmic Oz, as you call it. I'm not sure everyone has the desire, or the ability."

"But you feel it is your mission to bring that longing to life, to bring back jewels from the Emerald City as evidence that it exists."

"I suppose I do. Only the jewels in this case are ideas." I ask him why he feels such a desperate need to prove the existence of Oz.

"Because we need it," he says. "It may hold the answers to some of our most desperate questions. It is a world which can only be a world of ideas now, but may one day be the very reality we will live in. Ideas are life giving. We need new life in order to evolve."

"New life and new civilizations?"

"I think so."

"Is this place a state of mind?" I ask him.

"Yes. Or a state of perception, I think might be a better way to describe it."

"Peopled with beings and objects which existed prior to your entering that state?"

"Yes."

"Give me an example."

He gives me an appraising look, makes a decision.

"That's the first easy question you've asked me. And an easy answer: Spock."

. • .

For readers unfamiliar with the original series, Spock is a "half-breed": human and Vulcan. Vulcans are humanoids whose ancestors were a passionate and violent people. At one point in their history, the consequences of these traits almost drove the Vulcans to extinction. In order to survive, they developed a philosophy of self-control, which was based on the suppression of emotion and the supremacy of logic. To admit to feeling emotion is the ultimate shame in Vulcan culture. Spock, however, is only half Vulcan. His mother is a human, from Earth. And although he was given the same severe training as every other Vulcan child, it is as though he has twice the emotions and only half of the power to deal with them. He is, in this sense, an alien even unto himself: Only by sheer will and ceaseless effort is he able to function as a Vulcan. He is further impaired in his efforts by being the only Vulcan in a crew of predominantly Earth people whose warmth, humor, kindness, sorrows, and other feelings constantly threaten to undermine his fragile control. And because Vulcans are mildly telepathic by nature, Spock daily experiences a barrage of feelings that exhaust him. He is also subject to the physiological cycle of "pon farr," a kind of psychosexual heat that Vulcan males endure every seven years. The physical changes that this process initiates are fatal unless the male "bonds" (is mentally interlinked) with a mate with whom he is also sexually active.

.   •   .

"I don't remember when I first met Spock," Gene says, sitting in the garden at Bellagio Road, watching Majel clip roses. "Although I know when I thought I created him. But now, it seems as if he were always there. I . . ." He stops, as if weighing the importance of his next words. "I love Spock," he says after a long pause, and squints into the sun. "I'm in love with Spock." The air is very still. He remains motionless, except for his eyes, which follow Majel's movements like a tracking device. The tape runs on, recording silence, punctuated by the occasional bark of a dog, and the click of Majel's shoes on the paving stones. When she disappears into the house, laden with flowers, Gene turns. "Spock," he says. "Not Leonard."

"I know the difference."

He sighs. "Yes, well, I wish he did." His reverie seems to be melting, but before it is quite gone, he says something in a voice so low that I have to lean forward. When I hear what he says, I turn off the tape recorder, and we discuss his intense relationship with Leonard Nimoy—a conversation he asks me not to transcribe.[8]

"Tell me about your relationship with Spock."

He brightens. "Oh, *that* is a relationship. It's very profound. Very powerful. In some ways, Spock is my best friend. I have long conversations with him. We're both trying to figure out the same problems."

"Which are?"

"The meaning of the universe. Who we are. Why we're here. The time and space of it all. Where we're going, and how we can prepare ourselves for the journey. You see, the journey takes place—is taking place—whether we are prepared or not. At least, that's what Spock says."

"Do you agree with him? Might we not stop our own journey, just by being unprepared, stupid, short-sighted?"

"Yes, I used to think that—that we could annihilate ourselves if we weren't careful. End of species. But now I tend to agree with him. The journey is inevitable. Humans will evolve; what they evolve into is their own responsibility. But the journey is unstoppable. We may end up in a nightmare of our own making, but it won't be in the same timespace we are in—or heading towards, now."

"You don't think we'll end up in a nightmare, do you? I mean that seems inconsistent with your whole philosophy."

"Well, even I have lapses. But no, you're right, I do not believe the future is anything but positive, because we've already made that choice. I think technology will save us. And, I think our own goodness will save us."

"What is goodness?"

"Basic human decency. An inborn resistance to inflicting pain on ourselves, on others. An ability to nurture our children, to protect them, is a good example of innate human goodness. Our ability to feel sorry, to sympathize with others. The wish to help. These things are part of our nature. The conflict comes when our needs conflict with those of others. And, of course, when we don't recognize what our needs really are. But we're learning. A century ago, the mentally disturbed were treated with the utmost cruelty and callousness. And now, at least we recognize the need to care for them, to find ways to treat or prevent such illnesses. Goodness is the impulse to improve the health and happiness of the species. I think that's clear. It becomes less clear between individuals, especially when one person regards another as responsible for his or her happiness. Then you have people saying, Oh, you are not good to me, because I want this or that and you will not give it to me. That's bullshit. And there are a lot of conflicts about that. My meaning really refers to humanity as a whole. Individual conflicts don't really matter in that sense. It's the progress of the species that counts. Two neighbors may be at war with one another, but if we have just torn down the Berlin Wall, who cares?"

"Is goodness also not the avoidance of evil?"

"It is the avoidance, I think, of evil impulses in oneself, but no—it is the confrontation with evil that is good. Not the avoidance of it. But again, I'm speaking of humanity in general. People have to decide for themselves to avoid things, sometimes. Sometimes that's the only sensible thing to do."

"Do you forgive?"

"Oh, the questions you ask! Yes, I hope I can say that I forgive. I don't say that there will be no consequences of an act which may injure me, but I don't hold a grudge. I would be interested to know how you would answer that question."

"I don't know, Gene. There are so few things that really

matter to me—I can count them on the fingers of one hand.
Most injuries are petty annoyances. I just basically don't
care—on the deepest level, I mean. On the surface, I might
have a fit, but within a couple of days, or even a couple of
hours, it doesn't matter. Most of what matters to me is so
unlike what seems to matter to others—and so unperceivable
anyway, by anyone except my family, and one or two old
friends—that I am almost impossible to injure. It just doesn't
apply."

Gene's face is a study.

"You look like you're trying to decide whether to say
something or not," I remark.

"Yes, I am trying to decide. But as you've been honest
enough to say it, I will too. And I hope that you will explain
this in our book, because I care so deeply—and yet, what
you say is true. I don't care. I really don't." He looks surprised at himself and at me, then adds,"Well, not in that intense manner, about my own little unit of being. I think I fail
to recognize the significance of injury sometimes. I have
other things to care about. And, as you say, no one really
knows what matters or injures Gene Roddenberry, personally. And therefore, he is rarely really injured."

.   •   .

God is an entity in process of growth . . . good and evil are only
patterns which make experience and growth possible . . . no one ever
really gets hurt because all of this that happens is happening only to
that same great entity, and why worry about the "us" which is simply
a fragment of that great consciousness?

GENE RODDENBERRY, LETTER TO DR. CHARLES MUSÈS, 1985

.   •   .

The Conversation

"And so, what does forgiveness mean?"

"Well, I suppose it means that we assume people have reasons for what they do, and so they do it. And if that somehow affects us adversely, we keep away from them. Or rather we keep them away from us. But we do not do them harm or wish them ill. And neither do we allow them to interfere with us again. Forgiveness is one thing. Stupidity is another." He looks at me curiously. "You must be very . . . free."

"Aren't you?"

"Yes. But I don't know many humans who are. You must be a changeling."

"And how does one recognize a changeling, except by being one, oneself?"

"I told you," he laughs. "We are the same species."

"Speaking of changelings, you said that in some ways Spock is your best friend. What about in other ways?"

"In other ways, he's me."

It makes sense, I think. An alter ego. But I am wrong about this, I discover later.

"And when he's not you, who are you?"

"Oh, I'm Kirk. Captain Kirk."

.   •   .

Captain Kirk was Hamlet, the flawed hero. Gene told me that, early on. He modeled him on Captain Horatio Hornblower and he had characteristics of Hamlet, who knows what he has to do, but agonizes over it, feels—as Hornblower felt—that he had to put on a brave front for the sake of his crew, even though he felt that he really didn't have the requisite stuff, that he wasn't the sort of leader he felt he ought to be. He wasn't strong enough, and yet he had to be strong, because otherwise they would have no one to protect them. I think, looking back on it now, that Gene Roddenberry was Captain Kirk.

ROBERT H. JUSTMAN

.　●　.

"I remember reading somewhere," I remark, "not that it isn't obvious in the show, that you created Spock and Kirk as two halves of a whole. Would you still, upon reflection, say that that is true?"

"It's definitely true. It is a profound relationship. A love relationship. Each has what the other needs, in order to be a complete person. That relationship could be considered the essence of *Star Trek,* if you regard it as almost perfect contact between beings. I hesitate to say this for publication, because I don't want to be regarded as supporting the Kirk-and-Spock show. I don't. The other characters are very important. There is much more to *Star Trek* than Kirk and Spock. I'm just trying to indicate here that that relationship symbolizes on board the *Enterprise* what the mission of all of the characters is."

"Well, I can leave that statement out, if you like. Would you like me to?"

"No. Not if you include everything I've said. I want to make it clear that I'm not saying that *Star Trek* consists of Kirk and Spock, only that the depth of their relationship, their recognition of each other, is extraordinary—is something to be desired."

"Is that because both of them are you? Because if it is, you can't ask two people to have between them what one person has within himself."

"I think I can ask that of humanity," he says humbly and grandly at the same time. "I have such relationships with others. You do too. We've talked about your husband, your children. I can already see that you and Majel have a profound recognition of one another. And us. You and I . . . you and I find great solace, intimacy, familiar ground in one another. Perhaps because we're very similar. We may be in the early stages of such a beautiful friendship, but in twenty years' time, it won't be essentially any different. We may know more *about* each other, have had a few more experiences, but we will just confirm then what we know now. It has nothing to do with time. It has to do with capacity. And a kind of *chemistry* between people. You can't have that with everyone, but it's an ideal to work toward. Reaching great depths and great heights. I've known people for ten, twenty years whom I am happy to call friend, but wouldn't dream of having a real conversation with. Not in this manner. And not that I wouldn't. But it takes both people: both have to have the desire, the attraction, and the capacity. Star Trek's message is really to increase capacity, to become more open and less fearful about these things. To become all that we are capable of becoming. To really touch others, become others, and not to be afraid that you will lose yourself. And to have fun with that, to enjoy it, without surrendering who you are. These kinds of love approximate—they are not identical to—the relationship you have with yourself, but they require the same abilities: to know oneself, to know others. *These are precious abilities we possess, and it's a terrible thing to waste them,*" he says fiercely,

as if I were poised to fly out the door the next minute and
waste them. "And that is one of the reasons I say I am
sometimes Spock, even though I would have to generally
perceive myself as Kirk."

"You don't feel that you're a complete person, as just
Gene/Kirk."

"Oh no, no, not at all. I need Spock."

"Why?"

"Spock is, to me, the essence of evolution in a sense, just as
in another sense, of course, he's flawed. But he's a profound
thinker. His logic is nearly perfect. He's not distracted, he
doesn't excuse himself. He's very hard on himself, very disciplined. And he doesn't seek answers through emotion. He is
undistractable—tenacious. He doesn't procrastinate; he sees
a thing through, logically. He solves problems by refusing to
allow himself to do anything other than focus on the problem."

"What if the problem is an emotional one?"

"Ah, you see, there he is flawed. That's when he needs me.
We have long conversations about this very dichotomy. I've
written them down. I'll give them to you; they're around here
somewhere."9

· ● ·

Kirk and Spock were sort of dream images of myself. Two sides of me.
I definitely designed it as a love relationship. And I hope that for men
... who have been afraid of such relationships . . . that they [Spock and
Kirk] would encourage them to be able to feel love and affection, true
affection . . . love, friendship, and deep respect. That was the relationship I tried to draw. I think I also tried to draw a feeling of belief that

very few of us are complete unto ourselves. It's quite a lovely thing, anyplace, where two halves make a whole.

GENE RODDENBERRY, IN J. LICHTENBERG, S. MARSHAK, AND J. WINSTON, *"STAR TREK" LIVES!* (BANTAM, 1975), P. 152

. • .

Kirk and Spock, having been created as two halves of a whole, develop an electrifying relationship that has been the subject of essays, books, and poems. Leonard Nimoy, the actor who has portrayed Spock for over twenty-five years (and who at one point became so involved with the psyche of the character that it caused him emotional trauma), describes the relationship as a form of deeply personal interpretation:

> I've heard all of these theories about the Spock/Kirk relationship and many many more. Practically all of them contain a certain validity. . . . As an artist, I try not to anticipate all the various levels of a relationship, because I think if you do, you take the art out of it. . . . I think what it all boils down to is this: here's a man who knows something about me that nobody else knows. Here's a person who understands me in a way that no one else understands me. (*"Star Trek" Lives!*, pp. 75 and 142)

Others, who have studied Spock and Kirk, also emphasize the moral value of their bond:

> This Spock/Kirk relationship is . . . the fuel which sustains moral courage, the kind of courage that can drive a mere physical body beyond explainable limits. . . . Each of them triumphs alone. But then from the lonely pinnacles of success,

The Conversation

across the deep gorge that separates them, they exchange brief
smiles. . . . "Yes, I see you. I know what you've done, and I
know what it cost. And I know it was worth it." . . . This is
psychological visibility of the rarest and most precious sort. It
is the meaning of a friend who is worth the price of one's life.
(*"Star Trek" Lives!,* pp. 100 and 101)

. • .

"What if the problem is an imaginative one?" I ask him.
"I've always thought Spock lacked a certain quality of imagination."

"He does. He makes up for it somewhat in intuition,
though. And if you're going to ask me what the difference
is—I don't know. Intuition is for me that mysterious process
that goes beyond comprehensive, ordered thought. And suddenly you have that shining certainty that it is right, this
thing that you have not reasoned out, and you have to go
back and reason it out on a different time scale. I have known
things to be certain and have needed to prove to myself that
they are certain before I can tell somebody else. It's a flashlight in the dark—that you reveal a thing to yourself and you
ask, Oh no, that can't be! But it's there—and you know it.
Imagination is something else, something closer to that inspiration we were talking about before, an ability to bring
things back from a personal dreamworld and turn them into
reality."

"And where is Gene Roddenberry when Spock and Kirk
are both operative?"

"That's when he exists. That's when he really exists, in that
state of being I spoke of."

"Do you feel you exist outside that state?"

"Well, other people think so. Sometimes that's enough."

"No, it isn't."

"No, no, you're right. It isn't. What I mean to say is that my life is largely internal. As I suspect yours is. Of course I exist as Gene Roddenberry. That's who I am, here in this world. I do the things I do, and I have a good time doing them. I am a television producer. That demands great attention, application, being present to the daily world and the people in it. I love this world. I love its people. And when I present myself to this world, then that's who I am—outside. Inside, I am a great many things. I'm not just one person. As you are not. But that's what makes us creators. That's what makes us able to meet and to experience so many people *as they are*. And to enter into experiences that we couldn't otherwise have. If we were not multidimensional, we could never be writers. My good friend Arthur C. Clarke has that capacity. Only he keeps it more inside, I think, than I do. Ray Bradbury, another friend I admire very much, has that capacity. But most people I know aren't like that. And that's wonderful, too. That's just life in all its variety. But, humans have a great need to define themselves. I don't. I don't like to define myself, because as soon as I do, I realize that I have put limitations on how others perceive me."

"You call yourself a humanist. A Jeffersonian. A lot of things. That's definition. That cuts out a lot of other possibilities."

"I don't think I define myself as these things, though. I lend myself to them for as long as they work. I'm not one to belong to, to movements and such. I figured out long ago that my wavelength was a very complex wavelength which included things I said and did—and everything about me put out different signals, and that complexity of signals had to emanate from me."

The Conversation

"How do they reach other people? You mean only certain parts will reach other people who can accept them?"

"I will answer that with what you said is a favorite line of yours."

"What?"

" 'I don't know.' " He laughs ruefully at his inability to grasp his own complexity.

"Many people know me as exactly the opposite of how other people know me," he continues. "If you were to talk to my friends and colleagues, you would wonder, Why don't they know the Gene Roddenberry I know? With a few friends, a very few, I can be all the people I am, because they recognize me in all these personas. But people generally see me through the more narrow focus of their own experience. The more experience you have of yourself—your selves— the more likely it is that you will reflect that experience and draw others of a similar capacity to you. I mean internal experience, of course. I don't mean traveling and so on, although that could be a catalyst. I know people who travel a great deal and are still very unformed. And I know people who travel very little and are great—brilliant fountains of imagination and ideas."

"Like Isaac Asimov. He's afraid to fly on an airplane, and yet takes us on incredible journeys through space."

"Oh yes, Isaac is one of my good friends; he is one of those brilliant fountains. An incredible man. Do you know him?"

"No. We corresponded a couple of years ago, and in one of his notes to me, he described himself and his books as too cerebral for television. Which is what the network said to you about the first *Star Trek* pilot. I thought it was interesting, especially since he and I had been discussing the similarity between his robot Daneel, in *Caves of Steel,* and Spock."

"You were? How wonderful. Why?"

"Just for fun at the time, although later I wrote a paper about it."

"May I read it?"

"Sure. One of the things I loved in *The Next Generation* is how you incorporated Asimov's term 'positronic brain' when describing Data's system."

"Oh yes, you're one of the few people I know who recognize that. Several years ago I wrote to Isaac saying, Would you mind if I use the term 'positronic brain'? And he said, by all means."

"Well, it was very nice to see those two worlds come together. And nice to know that intelligent, creative people of such repute exchange bits of their worlds."

"Most of them that I have met feel that there's no point in saving stuff, because in their lifetime they will do dozens of such things and there's no reason to jealously guard it. I never found Asimov, or Clarke, or any of them answering any note of mine saying 'Oh no, King's X on that—I'm saving it.' Oh no."

"How much of Isaac Asimov is in Star Trek?"

"Quite a fair amount," he says, slowly, thinking it over as he speaks. "But I haven't—it is not a copy of any Isaac Asimov work, and it's not a copy of any Isaac Asimov theories, except those that I have adopted with regard to androids. You see, I think quite a useful way to treat androids—or to build androids—is to build them with the three laws of robotics.[10] It presents a sensible thing. There is as much of Isaac Asimov in Star Trek as there is of Arthur C. Clarke. And, I hope, some of the delightful wit of Ray Bradbury. Any writer that I read and approve, I'm going to borrow from, as I would from any research that I read and approve."

"Tell me about the creative evolution of Star Trek."

"I think I am beginning to know you, and so I think that you aren't asking a historical question—you don't want to know the history of the show."

"No, I know the history of the show. And that information is easily available to anyone else who wants to know about it. I mean, How was it impregnated? How was it born?"

"I like the images of impregnation and birth. We men often have difficulty applying those terms to ourselves. But we are all male and female inside. Some people recognize that—especially writers, which is why I think my most intimate friends are writers. Others have a terrible time with that notion. But to answer your question, and I don't think it is going to be an adequate answer: As those things happen, it sprung forth with rather full strength."

"Like Minerva, from the head of Jupiter."

"Quite like that. As a matter of fact, in addition to writing a script, I wrote a whole treatment of how Star Trek should work. I wrote what I saw in my place of, of contemplation. I guess it's that thing I said before: they were there. Perhaps I am an adoptive parent, to continue the analogy."

"Who are the original parents?"

"I don't know. That very loose definition of, of inspiration, I guess. I don't say that Star Trek was created in an instant. No. It evolved. And a good many people contributed to its evolution. But the overall idea came rather, well, it just came! You know, over the years, I've used several tricks, and it may mean that at different times you need different tricks to keep your mind working. One of my favorites is to concentrate on something about our world that annoys me, so that I get sufficiently moved, so that I want to write about how, in the Star Trek world, it's done differently. Those things usually have to deal with the things we talked about today: relationships and technology, and openness, and so on. I don't start writing immediately. I talk to friends. I try to put my mind to where theirs is. I try to find out what went wrong for them, or what may have gone very, very right. Having done that, I pursue that line, until I start thinking consecutively, in a pattern, until I seem to be connected with that mind. Not in a fancy way, but, just in a useful way." He stops and searches my face for a few seconds. "Anyway," he continues, "for instance, I know Spock so well that I have actually turned out pages of dialogue with me and Spock. And I say, Why do you think this way? And he answers. With Spock, it comes very close to telepathy. But that is because I am Spock. I have some very good Spock/Roddenberry writing which I've never published, and don't think I ever shall. It gave away a lot about us and our relationship." He stops again, cocks his head to one side, and smiles ruefully. "On the other hand, that's what we're doing, isn't it? I'd like you to read my Spock papers. And I promised I'd find them for you."

.   •   .

I never knew how his mind worked. What he said when he said it made absolute sense and he evidently had the ability to think large in no time. He was kind of—Spocky.

ROBERT H. JUSTMAN

.   •   .

He reminds me of Jupiter/Zeus, sometimes, sitting so still, always in the act of creation, always in the process of generation. Physically large, mentally vast, and cosmically quiet, he has a paradoxical presence, imperious and self-effacing, as though he were winking in and out of existence, in and out of time. And yet, he is an enormously busy man, with many claims on his time, even at this stage of his life, in which he is not well. When I ask him later what his schedule is for the next day, he says "Oh," in a surprised voice, "I want to serve *you.*" He remarks that he thinks we will spend many months together, in companionable silence, in vigorous conversation, on the set, in the house. Unstructured time, dreamtime.

.   •   .

We have only a few weeks left.

.   •   .

"I learned something from a person long ago," he continues. "When you've got free time, imagine emergencies that you will someday have to deal with. When you're taking a long flight, imagine this going wrong, or that going wrong."

I start laughing. He looks startled.

"I have enough trouble just being comfortable on an airplane, without imagining disasters," I tell him.

"But what would you do? What would be your first move?" he replies in genuine consternation. And adds as an afterthought, "It's a delightful game."

"Well," I am still laughing. "I don't know about 'delightful.' Useful, maybe."

"Oh, useful, yes. Very useful. It's delightful too. It's nothing more than a game that you play with yourself."

"But you're not afraid of airplanes."

The Conversation

"No."

"Well, I am."

"Well," he says convincingly, "you wouldn't be, after you'd played that game."

But he has survived the reality of that game. Having been on a plane that crashed in the Syrian desert in 1947, he may have been saved from reality by imagination.

.   •   .

It is a bright morning. We have been sitting by the pool, talking for two hours. He has been telling me stories of his childhood. We were both precocious and voracious readers as children, with heads full of heroes. I ask him who his are.

"Well, I have always said Captain Horatio Hornblower was a great hero of mine, and in some ways he still is. Yes, he is, and Sherlock Holmes. But I have found in so many, many people evidence of heroism, the ability to perform heroic acts, that I think I have people I admire, rather than heroes. Of course I retain those early heroes, Hornblower and—and, well, I was going to say President Lincoln, but if you're talking about my *real personal heroes,* I am surprised to find myself saying that they are all fictional characters."

"So are mine. Why is that, do you think?"

"Well, probably because we are idealists, you and I. No one can ever really live up to the heroic ideal, can they? And so, they have to be fictional."

"Oh, maybe. I was thinking more that when you read a book, you know a fictional character—you're inside his head—you know the way he thinks and feels. So you can be more certain that he is a hero inside, before you take him as a personal ideal. Whereas with living people, that isn't possible, at least not usually. There are a few exceptions."

"Yes, I think that's true for me too. Who are your exceptions?" he asks curiously.

"My dad. My husband. A couple of other people whom I've been fortunate enough to know well enough to understand an inner heroism. But the others are all fictional. One is a combination of both."

"How fascinating," he says. "A combination of both. Who?"

I look at him in exasperation.

"Oh," he says with a swift descent into shyness. "Thank you."

"Do you know," he says later on that afternoon, as if it were unthinkably wondrous that people should want to meet him, "I've been fortunate to have been able to meet most of my exceptions—the people who are real-life heroes to me—Arthur C. Clarke, and Asimov, and the fellows at NASA, and so many others—people who may not be as well known to you. In this respect, my dreams have come true. I think our heroes help define us, help us choose the attributes we wish to have, the qualities that may very well be within us, *are* within us or we wouldn't pick those particular people for heroes." He glances at a small *Enterprise* on his desk. "But Star Trek is what best defines me—*if* you see it for what it is."

"You are your own hero?"

"Yes, in a curious way. Because I create or, rather, develop the characters with qualities I may lack or lack strength in, and they become my heroes. Yes, in the sense that I am Star Trek, I am my own hero."

The Conversation

"You keep saying that. Is that really what you mean? I mean Star Trek is also the studio, the actors, directors, the script writers. It's a TV show."

"I see you're playing devil's advocate. I think you know exactly what I mean."

"You are Star Trek. And the TV show is a manifestation of Star Trek. A manifestation, in fact, of you?"

"Yes."

"Well, that's defining yourself, isn't it? The kind of thing you say you never do."

He smiles. "I'm hungry. Let's go get something to eat." We make our way through the house, slowly. Just before we reach the front door, he stops and looks down into my eyes.

"I really am Star Trek," he says quietly.

.   •   .

This self-identification with the entity he had created permeated our conversations. Whatever we said, wherever we went, whatever we did together and apart, it was an Angelus, ringing out regularly and with ponderous acclaim, acclaim, acclaim. And claiming all who would know him to seek him through this one phrase. I am Star Trek—a cri de coeur of surprising intensity. I am Star Trek—a generic, primordial, insistent refrain.

To hear it was to hear Catherine screaming into the moor wind, "I am Heathcliff"; to peer into the burning bush and listen through the ears of Moses: "I am Yahweh." I had watched the shows again and again, looking for him in his television world, pierced with advertisements, and exaggerations, touched with the secret that despite these flaws has kept millions glued to their sets for over twenty-five years. I

didn't find him or rather, what I found seemed to stop short
of the rumpled vigorous man whom so many called a
prophet, a messiah. I had been to conventions, of course,
watching what *seemed* to be, at times, a sad parade of people
seeking a kind of sustenance among the tee shirts, phasers,
memorabilia of all sorts, and had thought "Get a life," as William Shatner unkindly (and truthfully?) said on *Saturday Night
Live.* Or *was* this a life (or Life)—a media salvation for the
internally isolated? A prepackaged fifty-minute philosophy,
beginning with "love thy neighbor" and ending not with a
whimper, but with the Big Bang? It disturbed me, this insistence on definition—which he claimed he eschewed—this
convenient explanation for being. Something didn't fit.

I had posed a question a few days before, about which he
said he was still thinking. The question was this: "The words
'organized religion' seem to bring a little fire into your reflective, calm response to life. Why are you so against it? Isn't it
the same as organized Star Trek? There are sheep in every
facet of life." He said he would think about it, and now considers the question seriously on our way to lunch.

"I think you have a point," he says unwillingly. "It makes
me sad to see anyone latch onto anything for the wrong reasons. But you know, you have to look further than that.
Some of these wonderful people who wear uniforms and
Spock ears and so on—well, humans like symbols, memen-
tos of what they love, and while you or I may choose different symbols, or none at all, what we share with these fans is a
deep conviction of the value of the principles these symbols
represent. They are often the ones who know what Star Trek
really is. And some of these folks are just there to have a good
time. They dress up because they like to have fun with these
things, to feel like they are a part of a world that accepts

them. They're not misfits, as the media often makes out. They're people whose environment perhaps does not allow for some of the things we most treasure in Star Trek: individuality, difference, diversity. They may be at a stage in their life that makes them feel good to go to a convention. It's not a place of 'thou shalt nots.' The only 'thou shalt not' in Star Trek is interfering with anyone's right to be who they are. I don't say that there aren't some very sad and lonely people who go to conventions—some people may use it as an escape. But the great majority of fans go because it's fun. They meet other people who appreciate the Star Trek future. And they find a little encouragement to go off and explore something inside them, some dream they may not have a chance to discover any other way. And of course most of the people who watch *Star Trek* and appreciate it for what it is don't go to conventions—astronauts, professors, heads of government, scientists, thinkers, people like you who both think and dream. The difference between that and a religion is that in religion the dream is already created for them."

I open my mouth to argue, but he anticipates it. "We're all in different stages of realization," he says. "Besides, here we are."

The Hotel Bel Air always reminds me of a monastery—in its silent hushed reverence for its own gods. Corridors and arches, sanctuaries and silence protect its patrons from the mundane. It is beautiful, its outdoor patio canopied this July day with purple flowers that drift noiselessly onto the table. A solitary blossom comes to rest on Gene's head. This time, he lets me order. And as we wait for what is certain to be a perfect and picturesque lunch, I look around. Everyone crackles with awareness: eyes darting from table to table to see who is with whom and to speculate why. Gene looks only at the table and me, years of celebrity status having taught him that catching someone's eye is inadvisable if one wishes to remain uninterrupted.

"So, you are Star Trek," I say, admiring the flower perched on the rough silver thatch of his hair, like an unexpected Easter egg in a winter nest.

"Yes. And I can see that that statement annoys you, and I want to know why."

"Because it isn't enough. It's like holding out your arm or leg, pointing to it and saying, 'This is me—this defines who I am.' "

He smiles his charming smile. "Well, it isn't an arm or leg. It's my heart."

"That's the kind of statement which can be quoted forever and thrill thousands. And believe me, I know it's true. But there's something missing—a greater truth, perhaps. You can't sum yourself up in so small a package."

"SMALL?" he says, outraged, for an instant. Heads turn. He lowers his voice.

"Star Trek isn't small. It's a whole universe of possibility. It's, it's the greatest panorama of possibility we have on television today."

"On television, yes. But what happens to you when the studio doors close, when the TV is turned off? Who are you then: a blank screen?"

He looks at me keenly and starts to brush back his hair.

"Don't do that," I say quickly. He gives me a puzzled glance. "There's a flower on your head."

What he says next seems so typical of the man who is not Star Trek to me, that a lump rises in my throat.

"Oh," he smiles sweetly, with the air of having been given a gift. "How lovely."

The Conversation

Lunch is served, predictably pretty, a seductive artful blend of color, form, and illusion. The waiter glances briefly at Gene's head, then at me, in a slightly accusing manner. Gene intercepts the look, seemingly without raising his eyes from the plate. "She likes it there," he says, with the same sweet smile. If this were a movie, I think, that would be the cue for the waiter to raise his eyebrows, and exit with a slight air of disapproval. He does so.

"I thought you loved Star Trek," Gene remarks in no particular tone, picking up his fork.

"I do."

"Then . . ."

"But I don't define who I am by the fact that I love it. And I can't accept that you do. Instinctively, you don't refer to yourself as the creator of Star Trek. Other people do. But you always refer to yourself as a writer. What I'm trying to get to is who you are, beyond what you do. Otherwise, what I hear is that cinema character of Woody Allen's in *The Purple Rose of Cairo,* who when he jumps off the screen into real life, thinks a kiss is followed by a fadeout."

He leans back and starts to laugh. He laughs so heartily that slight frowns appear on the careful faces of those at nearby tables. It must be some kind of sacrilege, I think—a man with a flower on his head, laughing, in what amounts to church. The flower falls off.

"A kiss, followed by fadeout," he repeats. "Well, I certainly have never thought that!"

"You know what I mean."

"Followed by fadeout," he says again, still chuckling. "That's good." He begins to eat happily. "All right. Would it be better if I said 'Star Trek is me'?"

"It might be nearer the truth. Can we stop talking about

Star Trek, just for a little while, and start talking about you?"

"Oh, I would love to. But you know, I am a private man, and I am so used to giving public answers, that I suppose I keep forgetting that it really is me you're interested in. Most people are interested in me only because of Star Trek. And I'm happy that they are. I think I'm trying to be self-revealing, and I don't know how much, or how little, to say about myself. I think I must be more courageous, and perhaps it is time—of course, it is time—to say some things about myself that it may not have been right to say before. I'm sorry. What should I say? Help me."

"Why don't you tell me what it is, when you're not working on, thinking about, representing in any way, Star Trek, that you do think about."

He stops eating and looks away from me—out into the distance for so long that the lettuce starts to curl. When he finally turns back to me, his face is noticeably different.

"Majel," he says.

. • .

"I think about her all the time," he goes on, slowly, haltingly, listening carefully to his own words. "I daydream about her." He stops. "Nobody knows this." He picks up his fork, puts it down, lets his hands fall helplessly into his lap. "Are you going to— No, that's a stupid question. I'm sorry. Of course, you are."

"Not if you don't want me to."

He sighs. "Yes. Put it in. She deserves it." He adds, disconsolately, "And in any case, it's true."

"Why does it make you react so somberly to say such a lovely thing?"

"I don't know. Maybe because it is so private. Maybe because I've spent so much time convincing myself, and others, otherwise."

"I don't understand."

"Majel is . . ." A thousand expressions cross his face. He begins again. "Majel is . . . Do you know why I asked you to come and stay with us at the house?"

"Because we couldn't get any work done at the studio. Because you said if I were to paint a portrait of you in words, then I would need to live with you and your family, do the things you did, be with you in your private life."

"Yes. All those things. And something else."

"You said, 'I want you to meet my wife. She'll love you.' "

"Yes, and she does. She doesn't know it yet, but she does. But it wasn't just a conventional invitation. I also hoped you'd love her. Not just for her sake. I also have a selfish reason."

"Oh?"

"Yes, well, now can you see what I mean?"

"No."

"Alright. Finish my sentence: 'Majel is . . .' "

I open my mouth. A hundred words come to mind, perhaps a thousand. Instantly arising, instantly discarded. Nothing comes out.

"You see?" he says.

"But, Gene, you've been married to her for over twenty years. I've only known her a few weeks."

"Doesn't matter. I couldn't describe her twenty years ago, and I can't now. I was hoping you might."

"Why?"

"Because you . . . see things."

"What does this have to do with the way you think? Who you are?"

"It has everything to do with it. Everything. Oh, this is a very difficult thing."

I feel I am treading on private territory. I'm not here to write a tell-all book. I begin to retreat.

"Perhaps we can come back to this subject later," I begin.

"No," he says firmly. It sounds like an order. "No. This is something I have to say."

His left thumb begins to move rapidly across his index finger in a series of never-ending cycles. It is a gesture I have come to recognize as signaling deep unexpressed emotion. I had told him once it was his magic-lantern gesture—except that the genie always wants to get into the lamp rather than out of it.

"She was my best friend," he goes on. I notice the word "was" but do not say anything. "We were great friends you know, long before we were lovers." I nod, not wanting to voice any question, to engender any thought he prefers not to express. "We talked about everything. Including Star Trek. Especially Star Trek. She would sit with me for hours, discussing this character or that, and props, and so on. It was my world, not hers, and yet she shared it so intimately." He looks at me for a moment and sees in my face what I am thinking, answers it accurately. "Oh, but it was harder for her. As it would be for anyone. It was something I had thought up—it was a dream I had. This was not something she would naturally gravitate to—this crazy notion, this oddball guy. She made a terrible leap of faith in me—I mean 'terrible' in the archaic sense: wonderful, frightening. Into that cosmic Oz, as you like to call it. In a sense, she helped

88 form it—not create it—I did that, but shape it. And once she made that leap, she never looked back. She stood for whatever I stood for. I guess she became part of my dreamworld, which is why I said I daydream about her. Well, we all have our own private dreamworlds, don't we?"

"And?"

He looks at me levelly. "Sometimes," he says slowly, "sometimes . . . I feel . . . I can't get into hers."

. • .

Later, much later in our relationship, I will ask him, "Who besides you has done the most to develop the Star Trek world?" He will answer, "Majel."

. • .

"Who besides Gene has done the most to develop the Star Trek world?" Oh, Majel, of course. She was there from the beginning— she's still there. She's half the reason there is a fandom out there—and Gene's the other half.

WILLIAM WARE THEISS

Majel.

CHRISTOPHER KNOPF

Majel.

E. JACK NEUMAN

Well, Majel, of course.

ROBERT H. JUSTMAN

Majel. And she's never given enough credit.

A FRIEND WHO WISHED TO REMAIN UNNAMED

Majel, obviously. She was a major contributor to keeping *Star Trek* alive.

SAM ROLFE

. • .

I already know this, of course. Before deciding to do a book on Gene Roddenberry, I attended several conventions, watched many of the actors on stage, took notes, from a distance, while those who deigned to give autographs gave them. At each of these conventions, I asked fans who their favorite character was. The answers varied widely. When asked who their favorite actor or actress was, the universal favorite was Majel, and the most common reason given was "She *cares.*"

. • .

The waiter comes to ask if we need anything. Gene seems to wake up. He remembers his food and starts to eat. I feel a curious energy emanating from him, a surreality of hope and longing. It feels like a plea. It suddenly seems very, very important not to say anything. When, still in silence, we finish lunch, he shifts in his chair. "I'm very tired," he says. "Let's go home."

. • .

The Conversation

He takes a nap. Whenever I return from a visit to the Roddenberrys I sleep off and on for about twenty-four hours. We tire each other out, Gene and I. But while there, a kind of exhilaration replaces sleep. Contact. I go into the TV room to find Majel. "Oh, there you are," she says as though I were late for an appointment. "Come here. I'm going to show you how to make hats. You're finished with Gene, aren't you?" I think how impossible it is to ever be finished with Gene, and sit down obediently amidst a cacophony of beads, pins, glitter, glue. There are straw hats everywhere—plain, half finished, complete. She sells them at conventions and *Star Trek* cruises, I later find out, and am astonished. Why would a millionaire's wife spend hours making hats to sell at a price far below any hope of breaking even? I give a mental shrug, and just assume that she does it because she wants to. There doesn't seem to be any other reason. But there is. The fans like them. She holds up a completed hat. "See? This is what we're going to do. What do you think?"

"Tacky," I say, not thinking, and am instantly regretful.

Majel lets out a peal of laughter. "You're such a character," she exclaims delightedly. "Now look. First you cut a length of ribbon . . ."

"*I'm* a character?" I think to myself, watching her immediate, intense absorption in the task of explaining. Her movements are Data-like, syncopated, accurate, simulated, as though she were wearing someone else's body, and is not quite used to it. Her blouse is matted with cat hair, her legs mapped with scratches from the rose garden. There are two pairs of glasses on her wild head. She holds up a length of ribbon. "Isn't this pretty?" She looks up at me. There is glue on her face. "It's the eyes," I think. Enormous, luminous, intelligent, clear, they promise an entrance into that dream-world he can't find.

"What do you think about?" I ask her.

"Whatever I'm doing," she replies without hesitation. But I can see that she is canny, aware.

"What if you're not doing anything?"

"Oh, I'm always doing something," she says. "Now pay attention."

We work for a while. I am hopeless at the task. She speaks to me kindly and slowly as if to a child. "Now, bend this wire . . . now count these loops . . ." All the time her antennae are up, searching for a hidden motive in my question. She says nothing about it, but I know, somehow, that she will return to the question. She does.

"I *don't* think," she says. "I really don't. I'm not an intelligent person. I'm very shallow. I like being shallow. I like fun and laughter. I'm not serious like you . . . and Gene," she adds after a pause. On her face is a curious mixture of expressions. For some inexplicable reason, I remember a look on Spock's face, in "Amok Time," an unlikely combination of defiance, defense, dignity, fear. She pretends not to wait for my comment, rubs a nasty scratch on her leg.

We have known each other for a month. Or from birth. We are not yet sure which.

"Oh, I think that kind of camouflage is the creation of a very intelligent person," I say. "But nice try."

She flicks the television on, and snatches the hat away. "Oh dear, it's all wrinkled. You have to cut the ribbon so it *fits.*"

· • ·

The Conversation

Later that evening, after dinner, when the three of us are sitting in the TV room, she jumps up in the middle of a sentence long forgotten now. "You haven't seen my office, have you?"

"No."

"I want you to see it. Come with me."

"I don't let many people come down here," she continues as we make our way to the basement. "But I want you to see it." She flips on a light. We are in a jungle. Or a dream. The walls, the ceiling, the window shades, are painted in an astonishing mural of flora and fauna—intense color, form, and primeval energy. There is more clear space on the Sistine Chapel ceiling than in this profusion of paint. The eyes of animals wink at us from behind their mythical leaves. There is life everywhere. Her eyes turn green. They follow mine to the leopard-skin carpet. "Fake," she says righteously. "I'm an animal activist."

(A year later, her mother tries to give me a fur coat. "Majel won't let me wear it; it's just hanging in the closet. Would you like it?" I thank her, decline, and tell Majel later: "Give her a break—she's eighty-two. Those animals were probably killed before you were born."

"Well, they shouldn't have been," she retorts. "Go away. You're bothering me."

"But it's her, not you. And it's her coat."

"She can wear it. I just won't go anywhere with her when she does."

"Majel—"

"Look, if you *stand* for something, *you stand for it.*")

At this moment, we have not yet been through that year—that year of grief and mourning, private tears and public appearances, conversations and revelations—the year

following Gene's death, the year that makes this sisterly ex-
change possible. We sit down. I look uneasily over my shoulder. She laughs. "They don't bite. Gorgeous, isn't it?"

"Wild."

"That's the point."

I wonder what the point of this tête-à-tête will be. It is not long in coming. She begins to talk about Gene. What she says mirrors my earlier conversation with him. I feel that I have stepped from Oz into *The Jungle Book,* and ended up in *Through the Looking-Glass.* I feel certain that *Romeo and Juliet* is next. Suddenly her Data-like movements fall into grace. She inhabits herself for a few moments. Her hands move from gesticulation to repose. She puts them on her lap and then, in a series of never-ending circles, her thumb begins to move rapidly across her index finger. I look closely. Her right thumb. Mirror image.

She wants to make sure I know who he is, not to make a mistake and think that there is anything about him that is not justifiable—even beautiful. That whatever he says, he has a right to say. That if there is any criticism of her, he is right, if not in fact than in the stating of it. She lowers her head, as if for the guillotine, and begins to tell me why. I listen. There is innocence in her neck. What she says, I don't remember now. If I did, I would not record it. This is Gene's book. All I remember is that I have never witnessed such a curious lack of ego, and such self-abnegating love in all my life. "If Gene is Star Trek, then Majel is Gene" I will write in my notebook later that night, and not know why. In the middle of her litany, I stop her. "Majel, I don't know you well enough to be hearing this. I don't have the right."

I know this is a false statement before I have finished saying it.

The Conversation

"Yes you do," she says, echoing Gene's own words. "Chemistry gives you the right."

I do not tell her of our lunchtime conversation.

She never asks me.

. ● .

In the two years that followed these conversations, I have heard many pontificate on the marriage of Majel and Gene—each certain that she (for in each case it was a she) knew the inner workings of Gene's heart, and none of whom knew or had the slightest possibility of knowing Majel's. They seem curiously arrogant, possessive, jealous, insecure—and firmly attest that the marriage was a failure. I find out, in these two years, from his male friends, that this attitude typifies a few isolated incidents of friendship Gene drew to himself for his own, odd reasons—women who claim him as a badge of identification, as if he were a dog tag. It is for that reason that I first discarded their testimony, the second reason being what Gene said in the pages that follow. The substantive reason, of course, is that I lived with Majel and Gene, and their magnetic, obsessive, passionate, bonded love. True, the bond was frayed in spots, and it was obvious that to each that fraying was as raw, as painful as if it were the layers of tissue in their own skin. The efforts I saw between them to hold it together were almost too painful to watch, each of them stripping tissue from their wounds to graft onto the other, in fateful remorse. They opposed each other, at times, because they existed to each other. Had they been indifferent, they would have lived in peace.

One day Gene talks about Majel for nearly two hours. I think and think and think for months afterward about all that

he has said. What I end up with is this: Like many writers, he
carries a population around inside him—ideas, fancies, notions, characters, theories, possibilities, dreams. They buzz
constantly with opposing suggestions, contradictory
philosophies, conflicting needs. They make claims upon him,
demand of him that they be given life. They ask him questions he cannot answer, force him to confront his own limitations. He feels obligated to acknowledge their validity, to
give time and attention to their incessant needs and, what is
worse, far worse for him, is the need to make choices. In
every choice he makes, about which character will live and
which will be forever confined to the purgatory of partial
existence, he hears a scream from those who cannot be
brought to life. Every decision in favor of one is denial to
another. Choice is his nemesis, in life as well as art. It is the
hardest thing he has to do, he tells me. There is one word he
hates above all others. That word is "no."

.   •   .

Life, like writing, is making choices. You can never know what might
have been. It is a drama: you're in conflict with your environment, and
your environment consists of other people, and their needs. You consist of your needs. And there's the stuff of drama.

Robert H. Justman

.   •   .

I hear many stories from those who worked closely with
him. He has no trouble saying no to anything that will not be
of benefit to Star Trek. But he finds it almost impossible to
say no to people in a personal capacity. In fact, I am told
often, that task is one of the few he delegates. Several people
recount to me the same anecdote: Someone who had worked
in a minor capacity for several years on *Star Trek: The Next*

Generation asked Gene for a promotion. Gene had no intention of granting this request, but, because he liked the worker personally, was unable to say no. Instead, he sent the employee to see one of his co-producers, then immediately picked up the phone and called the producer on the set. "Say no," Gene instructed him.

In anything that does not touch Star Trek, "no" is a word that connects him to fear. He is afraid to say it. What might have been beckons him. In this, he is connected to Majel so deeply that in this two-hour monologue he calls her a saving grace, a metaphor which is not lost on me and which he hastily tries to change to another phrase. But he can find none. That is what she is. Brave in the face of "no," philosophical about what might have been. "She lives entirely in the present," he says.

"My body could have married anyone," he remarks, "but *I* had to marry Majel." I am again reminded of Woody Allen, who once said that his body was just something he used to carry his brain around in. When Gene says "I" he disembodies whatever constitutes that which he is from that which he appears to be. Clearly his detachment from himself is profound. He is the sort of person, who, if injured, will say "My leg is bleeding," rather than "I am bleeding." He attaches almost no importance to his body, except as an instrument of pleasure. It has no intrinsic value. When I ask him what it is about Majel that saves him, he begins a discourse on infinite diversity. I do not know yet what he means. In the months that follow, I will find out. In her, I will find a friend in whose sheer presence there is peace. But that will be in the future. Right now, he says, his own complexity tires him. Majel doesn't. She is free of that whimpering population inside, and because of that, he finds freedom in her.

The Conversation

What he draws from her is nothing he recognizes: it is the very lack of internal divisiveness in which he rests. He needs her, he tells me. He needs her to be who she is, and the one thing that he can count on is that she will always be it. She is real, he adds proudly, as if it were a virtue not to be imaginary—and looks puzzled that he said it. Of what that reality consists, he cannot define. He knows only that it somehow absorbs the infinite diversity boiling inside him. Others understand parts of him profoundly—satisfy one or several of the people he is inside. But only Majel makes that "terrible leap of faith," and stands for whatever he stands for, whether she understands it or not. Once, in this conversation, he mentions *Star Trek* fans. Only Majel really cares in the same way he cares about the humanity of fandom, he says.

.   •   .

How deeply she cares is evident to me a few months after Gene's death. We are sitting in Gene's study answering thousands of condolence letters that pour in daily from a bereaved world. Among them is a letter requesting something with Gene Roddenberry's signature on it, to be given away as a memento to someone at a memorial gathering of fans. In the corner are boxes of Starfleet certificates on which Gene's original signature has been reproduced. When it is suggested that one of these be sent, Majel refuses. "Those are *copies* of his signature, not his real signature," she says. Her personal assistant points out that fans are sensible people who realize that a man in Gene Roddenberry's position cannot spend hundreds of hours a week signing certificates, and that a reproduced autograph is acceptable. Majel is adamant. "Somewhere out there," she says, looking across Gene's desk, out the window, and into a world that only she sees, "is a person, a human being who will treasure this thing he or she has been given, believing it to be Gene's own writing. Someone who treasures *Gene*. And they are going to *get* Gene." She spends a good part of the afternoon hunting for an appropriate item. When several hours later she emerges with a scrap of paper on which for some reason Gene had written his name, she is quietly triumphant. "There!" she says. "This is *real*."

. • .

"We still haven't talked about fear," I say to Gene when I join him in the garden, the next day.

"What do you think about sex?" he asks.

"Is this another Gene Roddenberry diversionary tactic?"

"No. No. I would like to know. Because I have a statement to make about that, and I'd like to hear what you think."

"I think it is not an intimate act. It can be made intimate— by engaging in it with someone with whom you are already intimate, or becoming so. But in and of itself, it's a human function, like all other human functions, resembling hunger, I suppose, the most. I certainly don't think it is a way to achieve intimacy. I mean, eating can be an intimate act if it is with the right person. Or it can just be a way of filling a need to survive. Robert Heinlein created a culture in which eating was the most intimate act, and these little creatures go into cubicles, or recesses in the walls, and turn their backs on everyone else when they eat. That was in *Space Cadet,* one of my all-time favorite science fiction books."

"Do you know that that is one of the most significant books in my life?" he exclaims. "Let's talk about that next. But, what *do* you think intimacy is?"

"I think talking with someone, really communicating deeply, getting inside that other person is an intimate act."

"Well, getting inside someone is also sex."

"From a male point of view, yes. Intimacy is also letting someone enter you, not just at a level of warmth and good-will and friendship, not even of love—but at the core, the place one survives from. Sex is a *metaphor* of that kind of intimacy; it is not the intimacy itself. It's a physical manifestation, at best, of what you say Star Trek is all about: contact."

"Sex is a metaphor of intimacy, not the other way around?" He seems to want to be very sure of my meaning.

"As I see it, yes."

"I think that qualifies as a lovely statement. And I thought you might say something like that. It's something I've always believed. The separation of sex and intimacy between men and women is something I try to portray in *Star Trek*."

"Where? When? I haven't seen much evidence of it."

"Of course you have. It's there."

"If you mean Captain Kirk . . ."

"Oh, forget Kirk. I'm talking about *The Next Generation*. We have a very lovely possibility there between Riker and Deanna Troi. They are friends, first and foremost, and then they have this sexual component. And they can choose to utilize that component—act on it or not. But it's not a ro-mance. You must have noticed that. I hope it comes through."

"I think it does sometimes. But I thought I might be seeing something that wasn't there."

"Oh no. You're seeing what's there."

"But other times, it seems like a traditional romance."

"Well it's not supposed to be. I wrote it as a sort of proto-type relationship, a friendship between the opposite sexes carried to its fullest capacity."

The Conversation

"How does that differ from romance?"

"I think you've answered that question in what you said about sex, but you're probably not relating it to my statement. Romance is a product of not knowing each other. Friendship develops when you know each other. And then, if it's possible—and sadly, it usually isn't—you can have intimacy. Sexual or not. It doesn't matter. Sex is not germane to intimacy, as you said. Two men can be more intimate than a man and his wife. Or two women. Or a man and a woman who understand one another, perhaps share one another's dreams, but have no wish to live together or share their bodies with one another."

"Well, I don't think it's all that clear in the Riker/Troi case. It often looks awfully like plain old American Romance to me. I love the idea, but I think you did better with Kirk and Spock."[11]

"Well, that may be because it is easier for me. I myself am so intimate with them. And then, it's hard to portray non-physical intimacy between members of the opposite sex, especially between such attractive people. It can so easily look like what it isn't."

"So when do two people marry?"

"I think they don't, in a perfect world. I don't think there's that kind of mutual possession. Marriage in the form that it is now cannot possibly continue into the future. That's why we have so little of it in *Star Trek*."

"There is no marrying or giving in marriage in *Star Trek*—as in heaven, as your favorite book says?"

"Yes. I think if we all lived in my Star Trek world, it would be pretty close to heaven. You see, the studio executives and so on think that our people are single, so that there are romantic possibilities for them. So the audience can identify

with the current love interest, as they call it, each week. But
that was not my intention. My idea was to portray a world in
which people are developed enough as humans to be sufficient unto themselves, and in which they have a wonderful
world of human and alien contact to explore. They don't remain single, from my point of view, in order to satisfy some
romantic need on the part of the audience. And I hope that
the people who watch *Star Trek* may see something in this.
We also have many families on board—traditional families
and some nontraditional families, which we haven't had an
opportunity to bring out yet. But those are just choices, made
out of many possibilities. That's something I would really
like to get into more on our show." He adds thoughtfully,
"Of course, heroes on television, and in the movies, were traditionally never married—or even 'taken'—engaged and
so on. That's an old maxim. Oh, they always got the girl,
but . . ."

"When they do, the movie ends. Technicolor kiss."

"And fadeout." He laughs heartily. "Yes, the movie always
used to end just when it was getting interesting, from that
point of view. Things are somewhat different now, thank
God."

"How does this relate to your own life?"

"Oh, it does. I believe it. And within the bounds of what it
takes to maintain a happy marriage, it's what I do. I practice
what I preach. There may be times when I feel like 'dipping
my wick' and I do so. When it's right. When it feels good.
People may say, 'Oh that Gene Roddenberry. He's no good.
He's an unfaithful husband.' I say unfaithful to what?"

"Majel, surely."

"No. Not at all. People aren't concerned in their deepest
selves about Majel. They're concerned about themselves,

their rules and so on. They mean I am unfaithful to the ideal, *their ideal,* of marriage. They don't want to consider another ideal. They may be afraid. They may condemn me for breaking a vow they think I made. Whereas in fact, I didn't make it. I could never adhere to an agreement that deprived me of myself. Majel and I have our own agreement. I would be false, a false person, if I did make any other kind of agreement. And I would be a false person if my wife didn't know who I am, what I do."

"And is this 'wick dipping' ever an intimate act?"

"You mean, outside my marriage? No. I have varying degrees of friendship with people. I am involved in more kinds of love than I could possibly relate. But no, I can't say that I feel intimate, in the manner we are speaking of, with anyone with whom I enjoy that particular pleasure."

"What do you suppose they feel?"

"Oh, I suppose some of them feel they have been intimate with me. Perhaps their capacity is filled. Some of them may just like to feel that they've fucked Gene Roddenberry. And that's okay, too. But I've never given the impression that a roll in the sack is the key to Gene Roddenberry's soul. At least, I hope I haven't. And then, sometimes, you know, it's just a human thing you do. Someone feels lonely, or they need a bit of loving. Or they just need some confirmation that they can be someone who is attractive to someone else."

"So, at those times, it's a kindness—a service to the neglected, the lonely?"

"Yes, yes, I think it is. Sometimes it is. Other times it's simply a way to love life, to love the life in myself and the life, the humanity, in someone else. Some people may think that's just my way of justifying . . ."

"Is it?"

The Conversation

"No. I don't need to justify my actions in that regard."

"With whom are you most intimate?"

"Spock."

"Besides Spock. A real person."

"Spock is a real person to me. He doesn't always live in the world you and I inhabit, but he's a real person."

"Sorry. I'll rephrase the question. Besides Spock, with whom are you or have you been most intimate?"

"I don't think I can give one answer to that. There are several. Majel, certainly." He names a few others—all men. I begin to see that by intimacy, he means an ability to reach him, while he is reaching for something else. Or to reach into that something else with him.

"No women?" I ask.

"Oh, I love women. I am a fan of women. I have many wonderful female friends. But, as far as intimacy goes, they never seem to remain sufficiently detached."

"You definition of intimacy includes detachment?"

"You sound surprised. Doesn't yours? I would have thought, from our discussion at breakfast this morning, that it would."

"Yes it does, but so few people understand that the relationship between oneself and another is subordinate to the relationship between one and oneself."

"Well, I'm not 'so few people.' I'm so many people!" He laughs. "No. That merging is a wonderful thing. I seek it. But it is not something through which you live your life. Actually, a lot of people espouse these views. But they just can't do it. I don't know why, but they just can't. Perhaps most people need something that you and I find in ourselves. One of humanity's great failings, intimacy. And a hard question to answer with regard to myself."

The Conversation

"Would it help to ask who knows most about you—well, not you, your inner self?"

"Well, at the moment, I'd have to say you do."

"And when the moment has passed?"

"I didn't say 'for the moment.' I said 'at the moment.' It's all these questions you ask, these glorious, difficult, goddam questions. And the answers I have to come up with, have to somehow find, in order to be true to our purpose. And that is true of the answers we decide to publish—and the ones we don't." He smiles. "Of course, it's more complex than that. As I said, we may be of the same species. And don't ask me what species, because I don't know. But we may help each other find out. Oh yes, I think we will always remain wonderful, intimate friends. I'm counting on it."

"So am I, but you realize that when this is published, then whoever reads it will be, in effect, an intimate."

"How wonderful. What a thought. I will be an intimate of humanity. What a lovely—what a magnificent thing to contemplate. Thank you. I think I'll go and have a rest. I'd like to be by myself for a while and think about that. Thank you."

.   •   .

"I've thought about that last idea we had, and I'm a little blue," he says later that day.

"Why?"

"Well, it's the whole idea of contact, again. People are intimates because they reveal themselves to each other—or because they are capable of revealing themselves to each other, even if they don't choose to at first. That lovely notion of being an intimate of humanity only works if it is reciprocal, if humanity reveals itself to me."

The Conversation

"Don't they? I mean, humanity has been revealing itself to you—writing you letters and asking you questions in lecture halls for twenty-five years. And in your experience of life. And now you're answering back."

"Yes, that's true. I'm answering back, in the best way I know how, through writing—in this case, your writing, but my answers. On the other hand, I don't know how much of the private Gene Roddenberry I am ready to reveal. I don't mind telling anyone my *thoughts*—those thoughts that are the products of my logic. My opinions, if they want them, are readily available. My overall dreams for humanity are available to anyone. And I don't mind telling any person whom I would consider a friend my deeper thoughts, provided I think he is ready to hear them. What isn't available are some of the individual impulses and emotions I have. Or my private reasons for those deep thoughts, if they are deep. I also have to keep private the opinions I hold of others—the actors—and so on. My evaluation, my word, carries great power in this regard. And I don't want to hurt anyone. And," he reaches across and gives me a little kiss, "I want to thank you for turning off your recorder at these times. Most people wouldn't do that. They would want to own Gene Roddenberry. I am warmed by that . . . detachment."

"It's on now, you know."

"That's fine. That's okay." He is reflective for a few moments. "On the other hand, I *want* humanity to know *some* of my private motivations, if only to feel that they are entitled to their own. We can decide between us, you and I, which things I am willing to publish now. I want you to remember them all though. Someday, if you live a great many years longer than I, some of these things may be right to bring forward. In the meantime, we'll just talk."

The Conversation

. • .

He will be dead in four months. For twice that time, I cannot bear to listen to this tape.

. • .

"Let's talk about answering those letters," I say. "Assuming most of them are about *Star Trek,* how would you answer them? What would you say?"

"I'd say that I think the best thing that could happen is for *Star Trek* to go off the air."

"I don't think Paramount would agree with you, on that one."

"No, no, I'm sure they wouldn't. Neither do you, by the look on your face."

"I'm sure you'll explain it in a way that I'll end up agreeing with you, but it's hard to imagine."

"No, I don't think it is, if you think about it," he says. "But I'll explain. *Star Trek* and *Star Trek: The Next Generation* are television shows. They're two different shows, but they are *television shows,* as you are fond of pointing out. When I say 'Star Trek,' I'm often not talking about the shows. I'm talking about my dreamworld, my philosophy, the one I wanted to put on television. And I did, to a certain extent. I can't replicate my world on television because there are too many other considerations involved. It has to make money. It has to comply with current society's standards of decency, today's values. It can never really fully explore the good side of a supposedly bad thing—and that's what I like to do most. We have to creep around an issue, say, like drugs. We have to condemn them because society condemns them. I'd like our

people to go to a planet in which drugs were a way of life—
not with all the violence and misery attendant on them now, not as a problem, but a natural part of evolution. A planet, say, where the rainforests have not been raped by the ignorant, and the chemicals found in the plants are an enhancement to human consciousness."

"Where, after centuries of ingestion, they become part of the chemical structure of the body, and you have a seminaturally genetically enhanced race?"

"Oh, I hadn't got that far. Yes, that would be a path we could follow. And the things people do differently as a result of that, because they would see things differently. Because of the drugs. Things that perhaps violate our notions of family structure, or male and female, or even life itself. And the next step up from that plateau, and all the mistakes along the way—all the failures and the triumphs. Oh no, I couldn't do that now. First of all, you could never do it in a one-hour episodic format. And second, well, that's the difference between my Star Trek and *Star Trek,* you see. But, and here is the answer, they do converge—they overlap a great deal, they're both times or places, not where there are no problems, but where there are new problems. Or challenges. In both worlds, people are still people, but they have evolved just enough that they don't see color of skin or a belief system when they look at another human being. Or when they look at a person who is not a human being. They see what's inside—the hopes, the fears, the dreams, the struggles—the real person. The way your Little Prince does. They might not like that person—that's their prerogative—but they don't dislike him for such a terrible reason, just because he or she is simply different. They may properly dislike his ideology. They may dislike him because the chemistry between them just works that way. You see the point. They can look at someone and say, 'I don't like him, but I accept his right to live as he chooses. He does things that are not compatible with my way of thinking, but I accept his right to do them. And that may well be because he is from Andromeda or Vulcan, or Russia. It may very well be that there is something about that culture that I don't like. But I won't condemn him. I won't deny him freedom or food or safe passage. I won't deny him his right to worship whatever gods are important to him. I will respect him.' We don't look down on others, as inferior, in the Star Trek world, in either Star Trek world. We've evolved beyond that—"

"Wait. Wait. You're going to have to explain that. This view of tolerance needs to be explored a little more. You're liberal and tolerant—about racial equality, abortion, homosexuality, women's rights, sex, all the popular issues—but when you meet up with, say, a Baptist, for example, you will unhesitatingly condemn him to oblivion. You choose your points of tolerance very carefully. It seems to me that when you say you've evolved *beyond* something, that's just another way of saying that whatever you are *beyond,* or think you are, is by definition inferior, that your views are superior."

"Yes, I know. That is a danger," he replies. "It is also an evaluation of progress toward a goal. In, for example, the goal of racial equality, I condemn the Ku Klux Klan, for instance. I think my views are superior to theirs."

"Your cat's views are superior to theirs."

"But I wouldn't deny that individuals among them might have other qualities—good qualities. I wouldn't deny them food or housing either—or any other basic human right."

"You mentioned freedom. Is the Ku Klux Klan free to disseminate hatred?"

"Yes, they are if they are within the law. They are Americans. They have the right to say what they believe, however ignorant or unenlightened they may be. I reject their hatred completely. I oppose them completely. I reject their methods. I reject their reason for having such a cause. They don't even exist in my Star Trek dreamworld. There is no place for them in my philosophy. And my object in *Star Trek*, the television show, would be to prevent them or stop them and those they speak to from believing it."

"How? These things are learned, as the saying goes, at mother's knee. Or father's."

"I don't believe all the things I learned at my mother's knee."

"But you're not the average person."

"Oh," he answers dismissively, "I'm not so different from anyone else. I've had my share of being average. But even if you're right, those thousands of letters you mention are from people who say that they have unlearned some of the prejudices they learned in childhood—they have discovered tolerance or the value of peaceful coexistence or the meaning of friendship or this or that from *Star Trek*—some of the very things we are talking about. And as for Baptists, my family was Southern Baptist. I don't condemn them. I don't encourage people to condemn them."

"Well, religion in general, then. I've heard what you had to say about religion, about born-agains and evangelicals in particular. It doesn't sound very tolerant to me."

"Doesn't it? I'm sorry. I never meant to give that impression. If I did, then I will correct it. I condemn charlatans. I condemn false prophets. I condemn the effort to take away the power of rational decision, to drain people of their free will—and a hell of a lot of money in the bargain. And that doesn't just apply to those religions you mentioned. It applies to your religion, and all religions which use the notion of God as a weapon against humanity."

. • .

The kind of organized religion that infuriated Gene was exploitive. Human beings exploit. Human beings are the only species on earth that I know of who kill their own kind. Constantly.

ROBERT H. JUSTMAN

. • .

"Religion isn't rational, Gene. That's the basis for faith: the inability to prove anything by rational means. Like the existence of your dreamworld. What if people truly decide to engage in religious practices with the same willing suspension of disbelief as they do when they turn on *Star Trek?* To operate within it for aesthetic or meditative or even musical reasons? Or perhaps to incorporate fragments of theology, mythology even, into their lives for their own reasons. Not your reasons. Theirs."

"Do you think evangelists do that?"

"Me? No. I think they're all nuts. But I do not claim to be as tolerant as you. And I will go to a traditional Latin Mass, occasionally—for those and other reasons which have *nothing* to do with dogma. Nothing at all."

"Oh, there's no question that the Catholic Church is a very beautiful religion. An art form."

"Well, art may be as akin to beauty, as Keats said beauty was to truth—and therefore part of it."

"Yes, it may be. It very well may be," he says. "But it's not The Truth."

"So if religion engenders even *a* truth, how can you dismiss it?"

"Well, first of all, there is a very great difference among these religions you mentioned. There are degrees of idiocy. Some are less culpable than others. But I reject them all, because for most people—not for you, perhaps not for other intelligent people—but for most of these poor devils, it's nothing more than a substitute brain. And a very malfunctioning one. I don't dismiss the people who believe in this or that. I dismiss the structure and, more than that, the very idea of the system of the organized church."

"Then you deprive me of my right to daydream my way through a form of idiocy that I particularly like. You sound as evangelical as your opponents."

"That's a terrible statement to make."

"Give me a reason for retracting it. If you had the power, would you rid the world of churches?"

"Of course not. I would hope that they would go away of their own volition. That people would find it in themselves to write great music and gather and sing and look at lovely pictures and statues and such," he says with a fanciful air. "Or bow and kneel because they felt like it. Or do any of those other things I admire in Catholic and Jewish ceremonies."

"You can't just bow and kneel when you feel like it. It would be a nightmare: everyone popping up and down like groundhogs. It has to be disciplined, choreographed. You might as well go to the set tomorrow and tell Patrick and Michael and Gates—all of them—to sit when they felt like it and speak when they felt like it. Art requires form. Structure. You know that."

The Conversation

"I can't believe we're comparing *Star Trek* to a religious ceremony. You're driving me crazy."

.   •   .

Star Trek has evolved into a sort of secular parallel to the Catholic Mass. The words of the Mass remain constant but, heaven knows, the music keeps changing . . . religion without theology.

NICHOLAS MEYER, DIRECTOR OF *STAR TREK VI: THE UNDISCOVERED COUNTRY*

.   •   .

"If they have nothing else in common," I argue, "they are at least both art forms and by your own definition, they both exist to convey an ideology, however divergent. It's a valid comparison, for this argument."

"I know it is. That's what's driving me crazy. But in *Star Trek* we don't tell people *what* to think."

"It doesn't matter, on the premises we are discussing now: art and ideology. That's all we're comparing. How one imparts that ideology is a different argument. But you most certainly do tell people what to think. You tell them to love thy neighbor. You really do, Gene. That's a commandment if I ever heard one. You tell them that violence is wrong, that handicaps are acceptable, that unity is a better goal than divisiveness. All precepts I learned as part of Catholicism."

"No. We point out to them that the consequence of loving thy neighbor is that a more loving world results. They can choose to participate in the creation of that world or not. We tell them that violence breeds violence, and that doing unto

The Conversation

others as they would be done by produces very different results. We don't tell them that they must do this or that. And
you, in your Catholicism, did what most people do not do:
you took the principles to heart and left all the nonsense behind. You're unaffected by that nonsense. Most people aren't
so lucky."

"Oh, I'm affected by it. But I understand what it is. I understand the good side of that particular bad thing, if you want
to call it that. And I don't think you do; I really don't. Otherwise you wouldn't be so vehement. Look, all I am saying is
that you can't rid the world of something you don't even
understand well enough to oppose."

"And all I am saying is that I think your experience of religion is unique. Centuries of misery don't bear you out."

"Do you deny the right of people to choose their own
forms of misery? If you want to legalize drugs, you're offering that choice to millions. I mean why not the opiate of the
people as well as the heroin of the people?"

"Choice is the one thing I would never deny to anyone."

"Everyone always has a choice—always. And if they let
themselves be persuaded that they do not, then their choice
has been to be persuaded. What happens after that is their
own responsibility."

"But you see, that is the very point!" he almost shouts, ges-
ticulating wildly. His fingers are extraordinary, like ten
bright magic wands. "Yes, people always have a choice," he
continues. "And they also lack the means to know that they
have a choice. I think *that,* more than anything else, is what I
try to convey in these dramas—that they do."

"And if they do not choose what you choose, Gene? What
then?"

"Then I congratulate them for having chosen, if it is a real choice, and I wish that their choice may bring them great happiness."

"And you remind them that in the unlikely event that their choice is a bad one, they can always reverse it and maybe then they will be invited to join the Federation?"

"Yes. More or less, yes. And don't look at me like that. This is no different than your university refusing to admit those who are not yet qualified to undertake its work. It's a matter of readiness, not elitism. A matter of choosing a path that leads to something beautiful and meaningful for you, but only if it is a true choice—in which you grow closer to an understanding of yourself."

"So the cathedrals remain standing?"

"Certainly."

"Then I retract my statement."

"But I would discourage humanity from using them for their current purposes. I would discourage, not deny. Yvonne, I must personally condemn a system I see as deserving of condemnation."

"But you don't necessarily condemn the beliefs contained therein?"

"No. Not at all. In *Star Trek,* there is room for many beliefs, and there are many beautiful, helpful values contained in those beliefs. How could I condemn them?"

"By portraying the nature of tolerance as being confined to popular issues. By representing the bad guys as symbols of our current objects of derision. Religions. Rednecks. Conservatives. Studio executives. Lawrence Welk. Dan Quayle. I mean if tolerance is really operative, then you don't dismiss these people as people—you merely question their views. What are you laughing about?"

"Lawrence Welk and Dan Quayle. But of course I don't condemn them—or any of those you mentioned—as human beings. I really don't."

"The test of that is how well you understand them, how well they think you understand them. How you portray them, if you can count any of them among your friends, and how much they count in that humanity you say you love so much. The principle of tolerance is so deeply embedded in you, and therefore in *Star Trek,* that I want to examine it very, very carefully."

"Yes. I count many such people among my friends. Not extremists in any of those categories you mentioned, but some who have a bit of these things in their thinking. Some of them are extremely intelligent people. A few of whom I like very much, and with whom I happen to disagree on a number of issues."

"Can you ever say to yourself, or to Spock, that you learn anything from them? Or do you consider the learning to be all on their side?"

"You think I am arrogant?"

"I think you're an enigma. Arrogant and humble. A secret supporter of both the sacred and the profane. I know you're trying to take a stand here against what all people of conscience object to—coercion, ignorance, prejudice—but I don't think those vices are the province of one group. There is as much real smugness and real unkindness in liberalism as there is in any other group. I'm not trying to ascertain whether or not *you believe* in tolerance. I know you do—the whole principle of IDIC emanates from you[12]—but whether your object is also to transcend the self-congratulatory, the very natural pride inherent in believing that one is tolerant, is *beyond* something. It's like taking pride in being humble. And I guess what I'm asking is if humility ever takes precedence in these discussions with ideological opponents."

"You're not going to let me off the hook on this one, are you?"

"I don't think so."

"Okay, to answer your question, no. Humility does not take precedence in these cases. I know what I know—what's right for me. And that's why, in *Star Trek,* we don't go into these issues too much. We let our characters have their own beliefs, without examining them too closely, too often. When we do, I hope it's with some degree of openness, which is what I think you mean by humility in this regard."

"Don't go back to *Star Trek* yet. We're talking about you, personally. What is the use of openness if your mind is already made up?"

"Oh, it isn't. It isn't. My mind is never made up. I'm always hoping to find a new piece of the truth. I change constantly."

"Do you consider it possible that you could find a piece of the truth from someone whom you completely oppose? A reactionary? Some lunatic TV evangelist? A racist? How far does your personal tolerance extend?"

"I think it's possible. It wouldn't be one of their fundamental beliefs that I would take as my own, but I might find something in their thinking—something in them—that was better than something that was in me. I would be open to that possibility. What I can say is that I don't think I have ever known a truly despicable human being, although, boy, I've known some that come awfully close. I don't think there is anyone I could 'not love.' "

"Even studio executives?"

"Well, that would take some doing, in many cases. But I'm very serious when I say that if I could look into their lives, into their childhood, and see this influence or that pain, or this disappointment, then I could point out certain things that made them that way. I could give you a reason for the way they are. I *could* understand them."

"Can't you assume a reason?" I ask him.

"Yes, I can. And do, I think, on a large scale. If you look at humanity—their struggles just to grow up . . ."

"But I'm not talking about a large scale. It is very easy to be compassionate to humanity. It's far more difficult to be understanding of individuals."

"Yes, it is. I think you may be more compassionate than I. Perhaps it was those years as a nun. Perhaps it's just the way you are. And I don't condemn you to oblivion for your experience as a nun. Far from it. I embrace you, and therefore I embrace it in you. I don't know what the hell I'm embracing. I'm puzzled by it. I'm very puzzled by it. And I don't know how to connect that with you, with our particular intimacy, with your openness. It gives you something that I don't have. And would like to have."

"But then, you have never asked me my reasons for having been a nun. You may have simply dismissed them as unworthy even of opposition—or thought you knew what they were, which is worse. It never occurred to you, did it, that that very openness could have come from that experience as a nun?"

"Not in a million years. Did it?"

"Largely."

"How?"

I tell him.

"My God," he says when I am finished. "I love knowing

that. I really do. Would you like to write something about that for me? With me?"

"Sure. I'd love to. Now tell me why *Star Trek* should go off the air."

He is not listening.

" 'An incommensurable existence between content and form . . .' " he muses to himself. He looks up. "You did say that, didn't you?"

"Among other things."

"Yes, we'll have to write something about that . . . a real socio-organism. You see, I have always tended to look at movements and worry about them. You're right, though. Movements are made up of individuals. But I try. In *Star Trek* we always try to see the point of even the bad guys. There are no really bad guys. I think you'll find as the series goes on that even the Borg have a redeeming quality or two."

.   •   .

An antagonist does not have to be your enemy. That's another thing that Gene was careful to point out to people in his shows. Just because that person—that entity—is your antagonist, doesn't mean that he is bad. It means that he has different needs than you do. That's the heart of drama.

ROBERT H. JUSTMAN

.   •   .

"And so, why should *Star Trek* go off the air?"

"Well, it shouldn't right now. I think what I said was that the *best* thing that could happen is for *Star Trek* to go off the

air. It isn't, unfortunately, the time for that 'best thing.' That
was really only a half sentence, in order to shock you."

"It did. It would make a great *National Enquirer* headline, wouldn't it? Creator of *Star Trek* Hates Own Show."

"Yes, they would twist it around into something like that. I despise that kind of journalism."

"People buy it."

"Intelligent people don't buy it."

"And so, with drum-roll, what's the other half of the sentence?"

"Because it's no longer needed. When it becomes a reality. When we are living it instead of watching it. I'd love that. That would be my dream come true."

"And what would the executive producer of *Star Trek* do then?"

"Oh, he'd do something else. He's already thinking of doing something else. I'll tell you all about it at dinner."

. • .

We dance like this often, on the opposite sides of issues. Another day, we have an almost identical argument in reverse: he embracing my position—I, his. In fact, we have no position. We both believe in both sides, or neither, or elements of each. Or, really, as many sides as seem to make sense at the moment. And yet, something inside disturbs him, in the same way it disturbs me. We seem to care too little about what people stand for, would consort with both anarchists and kings. It is enough that they be interesting and not possessive. It is enough that we can recite to ourselves our own private ten commandments. Which we do. We made them up once in an attempt to define morality.

The Conversation

But he will not let me publish them. And so we move in a number of separate, distinct worlds, few of which know the existence of the others, none of which overlap, and feel comfortable in our separations, divisions, detachments. We feel free.

. • .

We have forgotten to talk about *Space Cadet,* I remind him as we sit waiting in the hall to go out. Dinner will be at Nicky Blair's that night. It is among his favorite restaurants, full of life and movement, assignations, deals. Beautiful women, interested men. Hunger of many kinds. Humanity. And the food is excellent. He will talk very little and have an argument with Majel on the way home. When we return, Majel disappears for a few minutes, and Gene says, "I guess you noticed that little disagreement I had with my wife."

I nod.

"I think of her as perfect," he says fiercely. "When I see that she's not, I get angry."

"But Gene, how can you be so stupid?" I start to say, and am suddenly horrified. I am standing in the home of the world-renowned, beloved Bird of the Galaxy, creator of *Star Trek,* futurist, visionary, genius, and friend, calling him stupid. I start to apologize.

"Don't," he says. "I *am* stupid about Majel."

. • .

Later that evening, in an enormous bedroom, which used to be Cary Grant's, I sit looking through my notebooks and thinking. So far, I notice, there are only three real answers to the questions I ask him: Humanity, Majel, and Spock. Somehow, these seem to add up to the overall answer, which is Star Trek, which in turn is a dreamworld, which, by his own definition is himself. I am unable to coalesce these streams of consciousness at this point, and so turn on the television. It is a documentary about a volcanic eruption. The molten earth pours into the sea. Fire burns on the water. I think of the argument. Water boils on the fire. New ground begins to form. Genesis. A world created by conflict. Water and fire. Pisces and Leo. Volcano. Vulcan. Spock. I go to bed.

· • ·

The next afternoon, I sit on the floor, resting against Gene's wheelchair, playing with one of the cats. Majel is lying on the couch, intermittently reading, watching a golf tournament, and eating gumdrops. "Have some," she says, throwing some in my direction. "They're really good." A few multicolored Gummy Bears come whizzing across Gene's lap. "Majel, don't throw candy at our friends," he says absently, as one hits me on the cheek.

"They're only two calories," she answers. I avoid Gene's eye. When she goes out to the kitchen a minute later, to get me some strange papaya to take home, we smile at each other. "I love these absurdities," I tell him. "Oh, she does it on purpose," he says. "It's wonderful. She keeps the universe straight for me."

I watch him for a few minutes after this exchange. We have no audible conversation. But I know where he is. He is in a new world in which the laws of physics are altered, a world where calories, energy, weight, velocity, mass, force, acceleration have new, interconnective properties of propulsion, and starships operate on gumdrop principles. The simplest statement from Majel will suddenly fling him into a new universe. I have seen it happen before. I will see it again.

. ● .

One thing we didn't discuss today is how Gene felt about Majel. He loved her. He loved her and he was proud of her. He was so happy with Majel. He would just light up when she was around. Majel was a very big part of his life, probably the greatest part of his personal life.

ROBERT H. JUSTMAN

. ● .

He gives me a phone number before I go home, asks me not to give it to anyone else, tells me a time to call him. When I do, he is there, and we go over what I have written. He eliminates one passage, changes his mind about something else. I rewrite it, read it to him, and he is happy. The rest stands. "I'm disturbed about something in my mind," he says.

"What's that?"

"Well, the limits of tolerance. I think I may be more narrow than I would like to be."

"Oh, I don't think so, Gene. It was just a debate. When you meet one of these ideological opponents, you sit and talk and open your heart—you always do."

"Yes," he says thoughtfully. "I think I do. I really do."

"It's just a case of hate the sin, love the sinner, whatever you consider that particular sin to be. As you said, there really isn't anyone you could not love."

"Oh, but I might not like them. I might be very happy that I don't have to deal with them."

The Conversation

"Yes, I know. But, as you also say, loving is helping. And maybe the best thing is to help them by not dealing with them, helping them to realize that one of the consequences of their particular beliefs is to be barred from enjoying a *real* friendship with people like you. Or," I add, by this time almost resigned to incorporating *Star Trek* into every conversation, "in the case of the show, from the Federation."

"You are marvelous," he says.

"I am marveling. I'm surprised that it's still bothering you. And I'm sorry. You are one of the most tolerant, loving people I know. I didn't mean to imply otherwise. I just want to know what it all means to you—to be so sure of yourself— as you always are."

"Not always," he says.

. • .

"I was not sure of myself . . . at first," he says haltingly. "I was certain that compared to others, my life was really a small and unimportant thing. As I reached a certain age, I began to think, well, maybe not really unimportant, but certainly less important than the rest of the world. And, and it's been a slow rise to accepting the fact that my life is important and is significant and is—good."

"When did you start to realize that?"

"It paralleled my success with *Star Trek*. Not that because of *Star Trek*, I was important, but that because of *Star Trek*, I had important things to say. I would say the last twelve years, I've been almost certain—no, I've been certain—that my life had meaning. But that certainty, well, it's not always there all of the time."

"What do you most depend on to get you through these times of uncertainty?"

"My imagination. I have lovely evenings with myself in which I dare the world to tell me otherwise."

"You reach reality, then, through imagination? Does something have to go through that process for you, in order to become real?"

"I think so, yes. Nothing is really real to me unless it also exists in my dreamworld."

. • .

He has a character called Gaan, an alien from an underwater world, who has come to earth in order to study humanity. He tells me a little about him, and after his death Majel gives me the treatment for the show which was to have been developed. Gaan, of course, is Gene, I recognize, as I read his observations on humanity. One thing he says reminds me of this conversation: "Until recently, humans have been preoccupied almost exclusively with their external world, believing material things are the only form of reality. The same error characterized their present step into space so far. But, fortunately, some of them are at last discovering the existence of inner space. And as they become familiar with inner space, humans will begin to understand, of course, that infinity extends not only outward, but in all directions."

. • .

In the same conversation, I ask him another question on my list: "What would you not want to lose?"

While he is thinking, I prepare to write down "Spock" or "my imagination" or some equally metaphysical answer. When his answer comes, I am unprepared.

The Conversation

"I think I would not like to lose—Ernie," he says.

"Ernie?"

"Yes, my personal assistant. That's right. You haven't met him, have you? He's away on vacation."

"Well, why wouldn't you like to lose Ernie?"

"I think it's because of something I really find I need these days—a kind of forethought, I would say. He is wonderful—he has a way of, he has something that leaves me free—to do the things I have to do, and not concern myself with the things I should be doing."

"Why wouldn't you be concerned about the things you should be doing?"

"Oh, I am concerned. But Ernie does them."

"Well, Gene, I hate to say this, but that's one of the chief exercises in a convent or monastery. It's called 'anticipating one's superiors.' "

"I don't consider myself superior to anyone."

"No, and you know I didn't mean that. But as a leader of any large physical and metaphysical concern, someone whose life is made up of a hundred details, the object is to get on with the major concern and not have to deal with all the components. And not have to constantly tell your assistant what to do with each of the details. It means that the assistant is astute and sensitive to the needs of the person he is assigned to—before those needs arise—he anticipates what it takes to help, to facilitate a large body of work."

"Oh yes. That's what I have in Ernie. And he agrees to belong to me for the time that he is with me. I know that *I* am his job. He is perfect—he understands that. It's a peaceful situation. He leaves me free."

Being left "free" is something to which he always returns. He is adamant about freedom. Sometimes it manifests in discussions about intimacy, another subject to which he involuntarily returns often; sometimes he incorporates the notion of freedom into the process of creativity. His greatest battles, both personal and global, have been between the conflicting need for contact and the preservation of freedom, and yet he never seems to come to a conclusion about the correct balance. He will talk about intimacy in terms of being left alone; he will talk about freedom as a vehicle for exploring intimacy; and more often than not, he mentions Hitler.

I know what he means, when he says that he admires Hitler. He does not, of course. What he admires is determination and industry and certain efficiencies that were introduced into Germany during the Third Reich. He admires the fierceness and focus with which an almost impossible task of recreating something devastated, almost dead, is successfully executed in the creation of something strong. One of the hallmarks of his thinking is to separate—to see something good embedded in an evil he once said he was happy to fight. He separates the motivation from the result and ends up musing about a system that if it were not designed to obliterate freedom, would facilitate it beyond imagining. I tell him about monastic life—whose motivation he surprisingly does not reject in this conversation—in which each day is designed to achieve maximum productivity and efficiency, so that one may be left free for study and contemplation, and whatever work one has undertaken to do. He concedes the point. We argue about metaphysics for a moment and return to Ernie.[13] These are the patterns of our conversations—random links in a chain that will soon connect us irrevocably. We have one more link to forge. The materials for this last bright circle are hidden in this phone conversation, and won't be called into use until our next meeting.

One day, in the middle of a discussion about "The City on the Edge of Forever," he decides to explain how airplanes work, draws pictures in the air with his beautiful hands. His descriptions are precise and practical. If the nature of humanity eludes him, the principles of aerodynamics do not. He is a former Pan American pilot, a bomber pilot in World War II. I listen carefully, though perplexed by the abrupt change of subject. When he has finished, I ask him why the tangent.

"You said last week that you were nervous about air travel," he reminds me.

"Yes . . ."

"I wanted to help."

· • ·

Undisputably the most popular episode of the original series, "The City on the Edge of Forever" is a study of help—and a poignant tribute to the heroic ideal. In this classic tragedy, Captain Kirk must allow, even facilitate, the death of the woman he loves (Edith Keeler, played by Joan Collins), in order to retrieve the destiny of Earth from an alternate timeline, in which the Nazis were victorious in World War II. This is one instance when "the needs of the many outweigh the needs of the few—or the one."

An ironic twist in this striking drama is marked by Kirk's well-known line, in response to Edith's plea that he let her help him: "Let me help. A hundred years or so from now, I believe, a famous novelist will write a classic using that theme. He'll recommend those three words, even over 'I love you.' " Kirk is powerless to help Edith or she, him. Their destinies lie on a grander scale.

He must act out of love, not for her, but for the universe, and she must die to prevent her personal future from destroying the future of all of humanity. It is a story of heroism at its most profound, and sacrifice at its highest price.

.   •   .

I find out later from several of his close friends that Gene himself was very much afraid of flying. I find that impossible to believe. "How can a Pan Am pilot be afraid of flying? How can a U.S. Air Corps bomber pilot sit, as one very old friend put it, terrified in his seat? I am sure they are either wrong or joking, until E. Jack Neuman addresses my objections seriously. "Oh, he was never afraid when *he* was flying the plane. Only when someone else was."

.   •   .

"Helping is loving," Gene says. He goes back to the idea of sexual service for a moment, and then on into a discussion about helping people in the entertainment industry. It is a minor mission of his to launch careers. He keeps an eye out for the promising, the inexperienced but talented; he promotes wherever possible, dispenses opportunity. He is proud of the team he has put together for *Star Trek,* and says so several times. Towards the end of the discussion, a shift appears. He is now talking about helping *Star Trek.* Always, always the show comes first. He displays that dismissive attitude he so admires in Spock, about even those whom he could help, if they would not contribute to his show. We go back to "The City on the Edge of Forever."

The Conversation

"I had a big fight with a writer about that episode. Harlan Ellison. Brilliant writer."

"What were you fighting about?"

"He turned in an episode which was a brilliant piece of work—if there had been no *Star Trek* pattern to follow. But by the time of this episode we had laid down who our people were: who Scotty was, and who the Doc was, and so on. Harlan treated it as though I had assigned him to do just a science fiction episode. And I told him that wasn't satisfactory. So, he futzed around with a rewrite. But he just never solved the basic problem of why are we doing this series. Who is Kirk? Who is Spock? And so I rewrote it. Completely. To the point where he angrily took his name off it."

"So on the credits, does it say written by Gene Roddenberry?"

"No, it does not. I made a rule that I wouldn't put my name on many episodes, even if I rewrote them entirely, as I so often did. I like to give credit to worthy ideas, to the person who brings them to my attention. It's the fans' favorite episode. And, oh, he didn't pursue that. It was pointed out to him that if he took his name off it, there was no reason that I shouldn't rewrite it if I wanted to and put my name on it. Because, clearly, I had changed the whole thing. It really rankled me, because he won the Writers Guild prize. And I made a complaint about that. I pointed out that if you were to take first drafts and submit them, there are many excellent episodes that could be submitted, but not fairly. Because it doesn't follow the pattern of what you guaranteed to write. And, we had a huge fight and he was as near a thing as I ever had as an enemy. He was a very proud writer. And the very fact that I had rewritten it really upset him. But it was obvious why I had to rewrite it: I had to put *our* people in."

"I understand that, but it would be hard for any writer.

Why not just say, 'No, this is not acceptable. Write some-thing else'?"

"No, because you lose a story, then. Why else is this accepted by the fans as one of the best episodes? As the favorite episode?"

"I don't know. It's not mine."

"It's well done, well acted. And I made the studio spend an extra twenty-five thousand on it, in the days when twenty-five thousand isn't what it is today. But there are many shows that I know which if the first draft were submitted, would win a prize too. In fact I made the Writers Guild change that rule. For television, it has to be the script that appears on the screen."

.   •   .

Gene rewrote everything. But the original writers got the credit.

ROBERT H. JUSTMAN

.   •   .

"It was certainly my favorite episode," Gene continues.

"Is it still?"

"Yes. What's yours?"

" 'The Empath,' I think. Not sure. Maybe 'Devil in the Dark.' "

"Well it happens to be close to something that is close to you. I love 'The Empath' too. It won an Emmy, you know."

"Yes. And that's odd because it's not a typical episode. But I can't name a favorite. I would give 'moment Emmys' to so many of them. Sometimes, in an average episode, there are spectacular performances, ideas, plots. There are so many scattered throughout the series."

"Well, the object is to get them all in one episode. Or all episodes. You don't look for perfection, then?"

"Not in television."

"Oh," he says, "well I do."

"I'm speaking as a viewer now. If I were responsible for creating a show, as you are, I think my answer would be different."

"I'm sure it would. Let me tell you about 'Devil in the Dark.'[14] At the first of *Star Trek,* one of our writers had written an episode that had a planet in it, where miners were mining things, and the writer had created something that I didn't like. It was a story of them discovering large nodules, and the writer just made them valuable, because they had some chemical composition or something we needed. And that was basically the story. It was basically a story of—of—"

"Greed?"

"Greed, yeah. It was Gene Coon who had written that story. And I said, 'Gene, I don't like your story. I'll tell you, it has traces of greed and so on in it, and I would like the story much better if these nodules were created by creatures, and they were eggs.'

"And he said, 'Jesus, Gene, that's a marvelous idea!' Because Gene Coon and I, we thought on the same lines constantly, and that was all part of the Star Trek tradition of our attitude toward other races. Up until that time, we hadn't really decided what our point of view on other races would be. And that became so successful—obviously something we had needed to do. It laid out the whole rule of treatment of others. This was really putting together a series, and beginning to state what the series was."

. • .

What Gene did that was so brilliant was this: We have our *Enterprise* crew in conflict with some bad folks who are out to destroy us. And what Gene does is show that they feel that we are out to destroy them. That they have as much right to exist as we do. There is a film, *All Quiet on the Western Front,* that showed American audiences that the Germans, who were their enemies during that war, were human beings, and they cared as much for life and living as we do. At the end, Lew Ayres, playing a German soldier, sees one bit of life, one bit of hope in this wasteland, in this battlefield. And he reaches out to pluck it—it's a flower, one little flower—and he's shot and killed. People felt bad when they saw that, but they learned something from that: that we're our own worst enemies sometimes. Everything, everyone has a right to live, a right to survive—and it's too bad that we're in conflict. That's what Gene did, with the show.

ROBERT H. JUSTMAN

. • .

"Yes," I answer, " 'The Devil in the Dark' has a lovely comment about peaceful coexistence between species that could so easily destroy each other. And quite an accurate portrayal of motherhood. I thought it was remarkable."

"Motherhood is important to you."

"As an understatement, that will do."

"Oh, the experience of parenthood is one of the most remarkable experiences," Gene says. "Feelings and instincts arise that—that you wouldn't have suspected. I always feel a little sorry for people who don't have the opportunity to be . . . transformed in this manner. They will always lack a vital human experience."

"And one that cannot be approximated by any other means. It always makes me shudder to hear people say, 'No, I don't have any children, but I have a cat'—or a dog."

"Yes, poor devils." He thinks for a moment. "What an insult to humanity."

.　●　.

"I want to say something more about helping," he says. "And I think it will answer some of the other questions I perhaps haven't answered as fully as I could. This is a very personal thing. I have told this story before, but I have a deep personal feeling about this that I'd like to convey now. It changed something inside Gene Roddenberry forever. And it has to do with Arthur C. Clarke."

He leans forward, with his eyes fixed over my shoulder, somewhere in 1969. "When *Star Trek* had its three-year run and was canceled a few weeks before humans landed on the moon," he begins, with a slight irony in his voice, "I was, I was—well I had hoped that *Star Trek* would endure. And Arthur C. Clarke, whom I had met and had corresponded with while I was doing *Star Trek,* was lecturing at an astronomy convention. And I made a special trip to hear him, and applaud him, and see him. And to express my disappointment that we hadn't done anything together. And I, I suppose I expressed a little displeasure and disappointment. And Arthur said, 'Oh, my God, I don't think you realize what you've done.' And he proceeded to talk about it in glowing terms, about how I had created something that most intelligent people believed would endure. But I wasn't really convinced. And Arthur said, 'What is your problem?' And I said, 'Well, Arthur, I just would like to be involved in something that is a success.' And he said, 'Well, God, you are a success!' And he said, 'I have a public-speaking company that I am involved in, and I'm sure they would love to hear from you.'

"I pooh-poohed it, but I did go by this company—it was on Fifth Avenue—and the man who was in charge of the company said, 'Arthur Clarke tells me you are a *producer*'— he said it like it was a dirty word." Gene wrinkles his nose and purses his lips as he continues. " 'A televis-i-on pro-doo-cer! And *he* thinks—and I don't know why—that people would *pay money* to hear you comment on your adventures as a television producer.' " Gene does a very funny imitation of this encounter, and we are both laughing as he continues.

"Anyway, I signed up and my first assignment was to go to a small college somewhere in the East. They had room for about four hundred people maximum to sit. And I started to say something to them like, This doesn't look like a big enough seating area for the people that indicate that they would like to hear me. And, well, it wasn't. Three thousand people showed up." He shakes his head. "And it went on to be six thousand and ten thousand, and more.

"I can't tell you what that did for me. You see, Arthur gave me something that I can't even thank him properly for, because nobody, not even he, knew how I felt when *Star Trek* was cancelled. I was devastated. And Arthur . . . *helped* me."

. . .

"A few days ago, in one of my lovely conversations with Spock," he says next, "I came away with a piece of advice. I'd

like to pass it on to you, and to anyone who reads this book.
He said that one of the great lessons humans have to learn is not to incorporate anything into oneself which will disintegrate one. That is the meaning of 'integrity'—a question you asked me a long time ago. You see how long it takes me to arrive at an answer sometimes? It is a relationship you have with yourself: integration, integrity. If anything else, any thought or emotion or person, tries to force its way into the space between you and yourself, they've got to go. Without regret, without remorse."

I ask him if he thinks this is consistent with a great love for humanity. He does not even see the connection. "Why would it not be?"

"Because it may do damage to someone else."

"There's nothing damaging about a closed door," he says. "People often damage themselves by beating themselves against it. That human yearning for intimacy carries them into places they have no right to be. It's the product of an adolescent species. They don't understand what it means to be intimate with themselves. How can they truly be intimate with another person? Or people. Spock has a lot to teach us about the maturing of the human race. I'm not responsible—and neither are you, neither is anyone—for anyone else's inability to grow up. We may feel sorry for them, we may try to help them, as far as we can. As far as it is right to do so. But in the end, it is that repeated beating against the door which finally makes people look at themselves. Isn't that something you once said to me?"

"Probably. And intimacy?" I ask.

"Comes, I think, only with those who understand that. Who have matured enough to understand that—or have not lost the maturity they had as children. That self-contained freedom of childhood. Otherwise, there is always that sense of loss over something that was never theirs in the first place. Great foolishness, and a great waste of time."

. • .

He treasures the childhood within him—more than anyone realizes, he tells me once, over a single, perfect, glowing glass of wine. Since I have been in such seclusion with him and Majel for many weeks at this point, this is not a surprise. There is so much evidence of this that it would seem impossible for anyone to think otherwise. He thinks about this for a moment and adds that maybe a few people realize this. When he mentions who these people are, I am not surprised to hear that except for his wife and mother, they are all writers, all men, and all over sixty. But I am surprised to see, when I meet them, how deeply that understanding is buried beneath a Hollywood persona in one instance, a military brusqueness in another, and an almost frightening intelligence in a third.

Gene spends much of his time in a wheelchair now, and often, when he is getting in or out of it, his shoes fall off. He wears beautiful shoes—all loafers—and when they slip off, we—Ernie, Majel, and I—have a hard time putting them back on for him. One day I bring him an ordinary shoehorn, having looked in vain for a more attractive model. His eyes light up. "This is the best present," he says. "It's the best, because it's thoughtful."

Whenever we go out after that, he shows me the shoehorn. "I keep it in my pocket all the time," he tells me happily. His natural childlike ability to appreciate small wonders, first evidenced to me by his pleasure in the flower that drifted onto his head at the Hotel Bel Air, becomes clearer as I spend more time with him. He likes to be read to, as he becomes less well; likes holding my and other friends' hands. He notices colors and textures with great pleasure. Once, when Ernie wheels him out to the car, he asks me if I like his shirt. I do. It has purple stripes and is obviously new. "It's a beautiful shirt," I tell him, and he is delighted. "It has your favorite color," he remarks, to my surprise. I don't remember having mentioned that. And he climbs into his Rolls Royce, in a thoughtfully donned shirt, treasuring a cheap plastic shoehorn, and starts to talk about the astrophysical theory of warp drive in the original series. I think it is at that moment I first realize I love him.

His own lovingness has always been apparent. He watches Majel with intense, absorbed pleasure as she moves around the house. "She's beautiful," he says to me once, with spontaneous joy, as if it were a new discovery. He points his finger to a distant part of the garden, where Majel is petting one of the dogs. "Look!" There is an artlessness about him that becomes more evident as we grow closer.

I buy a strange pair of shoes once—beaded and embroidered with operatic color and form. I show them to him in the box. He lifts them out, turns them over, holds them up to the light and says, "Magic shoes. How delightful."

"Yes," I say, "all I have to do is click them three times and I'll be back in Kansas."

"Oh, don't do that," he says. "Don't go away."

When he speaks of Spock now, I see that I was wrong. Spock is not an alter ego. He is what adults call "an imaginary friend." Gene just calls him friend. Sam Rolfe will tell me later that Gene's success lay in the fact that he did—or was—one thing: Star Trek. I see that I was wrong in this also, when I took exception to Gene's statement that he was

Star Trek. That "one thing" of which Sam spoke was a Kierkegaardian truth: "Purity of heart is to will one thing." Star Trek is my heart, Gene had said, and in the saying of it revealed the source of that unclouded vision of childhood he never seemed to have lost, a pure heart. In the vision—or stubbornness—of childhood, he has willed himself into being. He has willed Star Trek to be. He *is* Star Trek, in the same way that Spock is real, in the same way that Einstein insists on the supremacy of imagination over knowledge. I think about *"I am Star Trek,"* remember that he added *"if you see it for what it is."* And so I talk to him about its very core, ask him who he is when he says that. I expect him to answer "Spock." He does not. He says, "The Traveller."

In the first-season episode "Where No One Has Gone Before," a gentle, intriguing, sensitive alien (the Traveller) comes aboard the *Enterprise* to assist in an engine test. Suddenly, something goes awry. The ship is somewhere where no human has ever been before: a seemingly magical part of the universe where, as the alien explains, time, space, and thought converge. The crew find themselves unable to deal with their own thoughts, which quickly become reality, and are helpless to return the ship to its former position. Having expended his energy during the engine test, the Traveller is weakened to the point of death and cannot muster the force to return them to their own timespace. He tries to explain that controlling one's thoughts, in this dimension, means to control one's reality. Young Wesley Crusher, who has formed a bond with this mysterious being, aids in the Traveller's recovery, by the sheer energy of his friendship. As the crew concentrate their thoughts on the Traveller's task, they enable their own return, through him.

"Where No One Has Gone Before" is a stunning, evocative episode, full of dreams and questions about the nature of hu-

This is Star Trek philosophy at its best:

"Who are you? Or what?"

"I am a traveller."

"A traveller. What is your destination?"

"Destination?"

"Yes. What place are you trying to reach?"

"Ah—place, no—there is no specific place I wish to go."

"Then what is the purpose of your destination?"

"Curiosity."

"That's not an answer."

"I don't know if I can put this in terms you can understand."

"I believe that there may be a warp speed that can get us beyond galaxy M-33, but there is no velocity of any magnitude that can possibly bring us wherever this is. Is it true what our navigational sensors are telling us? Are we millions of light years away from where we were?"

"Yes."

"Well, what got us here?"

"Thought."

"Thought?"

"You do understand, don't you, that thought is the basis of all reality. The energy of thought, to put it in your terms, is very powerful."

"That's not an explanation."

"I have the ability to act like a lens which focuses thought."

"That's just so much nonsense. You're asking us to believe in magic."

"Well, yes, this could seem like magic to you."

"No, no, it actually makes sense to me. Only the power of thought could explain what has been happening. Especially out here."

"Thought is the essence of where you are now. You do understand the danger, don't you?"

"Chaos. What we think is what happens."

"It pains me I was so careless, Captain. My intent was only

The Conversation

to observe, not to cause this. You should not be here until your far, far distant future. Certainly not until you've learned control."

"You are from a different time, aren't you?"

"No, not exactly from another time. I—oh, well, as you understand the concept, yes, perhaps that term fits as well as any."

"And you have this ability to travel?"

"Yes."

"And others of your kind have the same ability?"

"Oh yes."

"Then why, in all our history, has there been no record of you or someone like you ever having visited us?"

"What wonderful arrogance. There has been no record because we have not visited you before."

"Why not?"

"Well, because, up until now, if you'll forgive this, you've been . . . uninteresting. It's only now that your life form merits serious attention. I'm sorry."

.   •   .

I talk to Majel about him, his paradoxical juxtaposition of man and child. He really is like that—something very few people see—she says, with tenderness in her face. She looks at me curiously. I tell her about my shoes, and Gene and going back to Kansas. "You're both nuts," she says, and doesn't know why I laugh. Or pretends not to. When I ask her if she's just "keeping the universe straight," she gives me a quick, intelligent smile. "Something like that," she says.

I realize what this phrase means the day of the earthquake. We are sitting at breakfast: Gene and Majel in rumpled matching bathrobes, me in my husband's shirt and an out-grown pair of my son's jeans. A few minutes after Majel goes

out of the kitchen, the floor begins to shake. Suddenly, there
is a loud noise and the chandelier starts swaying. Gene's arms
fly out, his hands splayed in a perfect Moro reflex. *"Majel!"*
he calls.

We hear a whoop from Majel in the other room. "Well,
that was fun, wasn't it?" she says, coming in to give Gene a
hug.

"Yes," he says, uncertainly.

"No," I say flatly, remembering the 1989 quake in the Bay
Area.

She reaches out from Gene's arms to give me a pat on the
shoulder. "Oh, lighten up," she says, glancing at his face.
Later I find her watching the news anxiously to see if anyone
has been hurt.

I read somewhere that very few people retain their Moro
reflex, and I wonder if it is a characteristic of the highly creative to retain the instincts of infants—to preserve a certain
primate response, which may mean that other, less obvious
inheritances of the human condition also remain. I find no
further information about it, but it is something that keeps
coming to mind.

.   •   .

"What is your favorite feeling?" I ask him once on the way
to the studio.

"Oh, I love the whole realm of human emotions. I love
experiencing them all, even the unpleasant ones. They all
have something to teach us."

"Right, but what is your favorite feeling?"

He looks at me sharply, recognizes the repetition as a
pattern in his own mind: insistence, consistence, the duel

The Conversation

between focus and expansion. A small smile touches his lips.

"Pick one?"

"One."

"Longing."

. • .

There is a glass of water on the table between us, half empty, half full. The football game is on. Ricky, one of three household cats (and named after Rick Berman, then the producer of *Star Trek: The Next Generation*), sits in the window, feigning disinterest in a flock of birds. We have been speaking of water, toying with the age-old measuring stick of optimism.

"And so you think the glass is half empty," he says, idly, his eyes on the screen.

"I do."

"I am more of an optimist," he replies. "I would say the opposite."

"I don't see how that is more optimistic. If the glass began empty, surely it is an optimistic statement to say that it is less so."

"It may be," he answers, and falls silent.

I sense a "but."

"But," he continues, when the commercial comes on, "if I say it is half full, I am indicating its potential to become full."

"And how does what I said deny that?"

"Oh, it doesn't. At least, not necessarily. But it might. It depends."

"On?"

"On how one feels about empty and full."

The cat presses against the window. Gene watches him.

The Conversation

"If the water has been half consumed, then it is diminish-
ing. If it has just been filled to half its capacity, it may be
awaiting more liquid. In either case, it is at midpoint, and the
same amount of water is present," I tell him.

"That's Spock logic," he says. "Infallible, but not the
point."

"What is the point?"

"Relativity. One of your favorite subjects. And mine."

The cat makes a lunge for the birds, but stops before he
hits the window.

"So the question is, To what end is the amount of water
relative?"

"That's what I'm trying to get at."

"Well, I don't know, Gene. It would seem to matter how
thirsty you were."

"Oh, I'm always thirsty," he says. "I like being thirsty."

. • .

He keeps himself on the edge of longing—a thin, waver-
ing line between emotion and response, between thought
and initiation, between reality and dreams. Longing is what
feeds his creativity, he says later: an extended foreplay with
the universe, a perpetual mating ritual. He describes it as a
terrible hunger. He describes it as an insatiable thirst. I remember a line from a very early *Star Trek* episode, "Charlie
X." A young man looks at a girl and says, "When I see you, I
feel hungry all over." He is delighted with that line, had forgotten it, repeats it with satisfaction. That's how it is with
ideas, he says. Never a girl. The hunger for a female comes
very definitely from one part of him, he says. He is in love
with the process of longing, with being hungry, thirsty all

over, a dance between starvation and satiety. He insists that ideas come to meet him in this dance—that he does not generate them, but only responds to their seduction; that it is not reason which finally hurls him into the creative process, but mutual attraction. He says "I don't know" so many times that we conclude there can be no more questions. He decides instead to take me somewhere.

"Let's play a game," he suggests. "Shut the door."

When I do so, he closes his eyes. He says nothing. I wait.

"I don't know where you are," I say finally.

"Find me."

I think. Where in all the vast universe of his mind can he be? I think further, but come up with nothing. I do not inhabit his world yet, and have no homing instinct. I look for him in a script he had said he was thinking about, then in the character of Picard, which formed much of the morning's conversation. Possible planets, issues, ethics, qualities, notions, ideas, and fancies. He seems to be everywhere. It is a clue. He is immensely quiet, but not asleep. I have seen him sleeping, and this is not the face of the operative subconscious. It is an intensely conscious face. I look around. The painting on the wall seems larger. It is a Michael David Ward print, filled with stars. Finally, I close my eyes. What I say next surprises me. "Warp 10."[15] I open my eyes. His are still closed.

"Why do you say that?" he asks in a perfectly normal voice.

I give the only answer I have: "I don't know."

"Well, then," he replies, opening his eyes and sitting up a little straighter. "*Now* is the time to think. That's the place I always start. I start at 'I don't know.' What just happened was not thinking. I do a lot of not thinking. Then when an idea

or a person or a picture comes to me, I think about it. Let's
think about why you said 'Warp 10.' "

"Not because of speed," I say. "Theoretically, warping isn't speed."

"No, it's not."

"And Warp 10 isn't possible, for a spaceship."

"I'm not a spaceship. But go on."

"Warp 10 is the factor in which all points in the universe occupy the same timespace."

"Is it?"

"I think so."

"Well, never mind," he says. "I'm sure it is, but it's what that represents to you that's important in my mind game."

"It represents timespace. The point of perfect union. I think I was prompted by your painting to look for you in every corner of the cosmos, and I had a fleeting thought—no, impression—that if that's where you were traveling in your mind, then I would need to engage a sort of mental Warp 10 in order to simultaneously look at time and space—that is, the time you might be entering, the future or the past, whatever you were thinking about, and wherever place you were."

"Covering all possibilities," Gene says with approval.

"I guess so. Where were you?"

"It doesn't matter. It's all relative. It was just a way of demonstrating the creative process. You could take that thought you had and turn it into a marvelous story."

"Where were you?"

"Let's try it again. This time, I'll look for you and see what I come up with."

"Where were you?"

"Oh," he says, "where you found me."

The Conversation

He was where everybody found him, as he would often say. With a ubiquitous capacity for metamorphosis, a penchant for camouflage, profoundly honest and manifestly evasive, neither of which words seemed to mean to him what they meant to anyone else, he took refuge in numbers: "humanity" instead of "individuals," "Star Trek" instead of "me." We play the game several times during our brief time on earth together. Each repetition of form produces a different content. It becomes an invaluable source of communication when he is no longer able to hold long conversations. "Find me" is all he needs to say. And there is always something—someone—in him to find. I have heard it said by those who should know better that Gene told each person what he or she wanted most to hear. While in some cases that was undoubtedly true, it is an inadequate assessment of his way of responding to people. He was a multifaceted human being—not false, but when confronted with an idea that captured his fancy, he would search his internal repertoire to find one facet of himself that was similar to his companion's. If he could find no such similarity, then Gene Roddenberry, with all his force, came into view. We certainly argued enough. And if it had been his design to tell me what I wanted to hear, then he failed. I never knew what I wanted to hear, and therefore, he never knew how to find it. He tried, sometimes. Succeeded once or twice. Telephoned me in remorse or revision within twenty-four hours of my arriving home in order to discuss it further. In one of our strange, synoptic conversations, several weeks before, I had asked him who he would be if he could be someone else for one day.

"It never occurred to me that there *was* anyone else," he answered laughing, but only half joking.

"Come on. If you had to."

Majel walked in at this point, bearing a plate of peculiar fruit. "Hi."

"Hi. If you weren't yourself, who would you like to be?"

"Um, if I weren't myself, who would I like to be?"

"Yes."

"Here, have some of this. You've never had it before." She offered a dish of yellow cubes, looking remarkably like those rubbery food squares the crew ate in the first season of *Star Trek*.

"How do you know I've never had it before?" I asked.

"Because you haven't. It doesn't grow anywhere else. It's a strange form of papaya that sort of drops off the trees up there on the hill."

I think how appropriate it is that something grows on Roddenberry land that grows nowhere else, while she considers the question.

"If I weren't me, who would I like to be? Nobody. I can't think of anyone I'd like to be."

"Well, just for a day, then. One day."

"I'd like to be a movie star—but that would have to be *me* who was it, not somebody else. No, there's no one."

I can't believe that anyone would deny himself or herself that experience. Gene and Majel read my face and laugh.

"I told her the same thing," Gene says to Majel. "Odd, that we both had the same answer."

They look at each other and laugh again, as if at some private joke, and Majel walks down the hall.

"I can't imagine that anyone would pass up that experience," I tell him.

The Conversation

"Oh, you would make an excellent casting suggestion. You probably think more like an actress than Majel does."

"I am an actress," I say. "I just don't act in movies. I act in real life."

"Well, that's exactly why I said I don't need to be anyone else for a day. I already am. Despite what I have said about actors and actresses, that was a compliment I gave you, you know."

"No, I didn't. But thank you. And why?"

"Because I think it is very important to enter into experiences as if you were part of them. To become other people, to act out different roles. I've always done that. And it has always served me well."

"But you wouldn't call yourself an actor."

"I think I just have. All the world's a stage, isn't it?"

"Is that dishonest, do you think?"

"No, everybody acts. The dishonesty of people is in not admitting it. How else do you learn—to be a baseball player, an airline pilot, a friend? You act as though you were. You take on the properties of whatever that role or that relationship requires. And you become so. Or you don't, if it doesn't work out. I am a very different person in private than I am in public. That's a simplistic division—it's just one of many. As you know."

"No, I don't know. I've never seen you in public."

"That's right, you haven't, have you? And so—good. You are not blinded by that."

"Might I be blinded by that very fact? If your public self is just as real?"

"No, I don't think so. My public self is real. But it is a reality I have created. My private self is—is just what you see. I may choose to be my public self in a private situation, with someone I don't know well. I'm still Gene Rodden-berry, but I don't present all of Gene Roddenberry to every-one. Or anyone. I don't even know if I could. I'm still explor-ing myself. I'm still finding out some things I can be. It's the human adventure. That's why children play. That's why adults change jobs, or relationships, or take up new interests: to explore the vast possibilities of who they are. I *am* the things I try to be, while I am trying. I'm sure you are too. And if it works out, fine. Then that new thing becomes a part of me. I think you're disturbed over a word you're probably going to bring up next: sincerity."

"I was going to say 'authenticity.' "

"Okay, let's talk about that."

"You talk. I'll listen."

"I think the core of who a person is remains steady," Gene says thoughtfully. "If you are a shy person, then you'll be a shy cop, a shy airline pilot, a shy writer. You might hide that shyness—you may even overcome it—but you carry the shyness and the ability to overcome it into your various roles. If you're an intellectual, you'll always think that way. It will be of service to you in some situations and not in others. There are times when it might do you harm. But you'll still have that way of thinking, that way of looking at life, in whatever you do. People judge other people on such superfi-cial ground that they are very quick to call someone a hypo-crite when they come up against a side of them they hadn't seen before, or are not equipped to deal with. I've been called a hypocrite on flimsier ground than even that—because I saw two sides of an issue when someone wanted me to see one."

"It is said that the mark of a genius is to hold two opposing opinions at the same time," I say.

The Conversation

"Then I must be the smartest man that ever lived. I hold dozens of opinions on dozens of issues all the time," he says with a laugh.

Somehow, it does not seem entirely implausible.

"And so, when you are called a hypocrite, what do you do?"

"Do? Nothing of course."

"What if it is a friend whose goodwill you covet, whose respect you would like to keep?"

"I think you can be pretty sure that if someone seriously calls you a hypocrite, then he or she is not a friend. Besides, that rarely happens. There are so few people who know more than three or four compatible sides of me, at most."

"Rarely. But it does. Has."

"Yes. Well, then, I am sorry for their limitations, and I go my way and they go theirs."

"Does that bother you?"

"No."

"Does it bother them?"

"Probably. I'll tell you something that bothers me. Now that I have achieved some measure of success, certain people allow from me what they would never accept from others. Because I am Gene Roddenberry. That's hypocritical. Oh, they may spar with me a little bit—a little bit—they're very careful not to do it too much. But they do not allow others the same freedom with them. I mean, Who the fuck is Gene Roddenberry? He's a guy. If I weren't famous, I'd still be that same guy, maybe sitting next to them in a bar. We'd strike up a conversation, and I would express the same opinions, and guess what? I'd get punched in the nose."

"How do you reconcile all your selves?"

"I don't. I know who I am. How do you?"

"Same answer. It just doesn't bother me."

"That would be the rest of my answer, too," he says. "It just doesn't bother me."

"But it might bother others."

"Well then, you just have to say what I say in those instances."

"What?"

"Fuck 'em."

.   •   .

"Tell me about success," I say.

"What about it?"

"Do you think success emasculates one in some way?"

"No. The opposite."

"The opposite?"

"Yes."

"How?"

"Success is a process of seeking answers for yourself. Every time you seek an answer and find an answer, you grow a little further. There's nothing in the seeking of answers and the finding of answers that diminishes you. Because when you find an answer and then later find out it is a wrong answer, you are persuaded that there are other things that you don't know. And it does not in any way diminish you. All it does is rule out certain things that in your past foolishness you thought were right but were wrong. And that gives you the direction to seek further."

"Yes," I say, "that's internal success. But as far as external success goes, often when people become more successful, they become less human. Less . . . nice."

"Well that is a judgment they make on the world."

The Conversation

"*They* make?"

"Yes, they become less nice, some of them, because they have decided that niceness will really fuck you up. Stand in your way of really achieving other successes too."

"Do you think that's true?"

"For some people in some ways. Not for me, because I adjust to that."

"You mean you're just as nice as you used to be?"

"Oh yeah. Nicer."

"Why nicer?"

"Well, for one thing, the longer I live, the more I discover about humanity's weaknesses, and learn to forgive. I understand why they are weak. I learn to understand it. I am so much a nicer person than I was as a young man. How can I be anything other? When I see the foolishness of people for almost seventy years—and learn from the foolishness of people—how can I not be a better person, having learned from those things?"

"Well, by becoming bitter. People often get frustrated when they see the foolishness of others, as you call it."

"Oh, then they're not reading it properly. What would bitterness be in that case? That there are things that force us in the way we don't want to go? Bullshit! That person is not reading the lessons of life properly. I don't promise you that every decision I make will be a right decision. But I do promise you that every decision I make will be more right than past decisions! And there may be a great gap there—between the correct decisions—but I'm inching up. And that's why I say that I am a much more pleasant person than I was."

"Do you think everyone else will say that about you too?"

"No. Some persons have been attracted to false paths."

. • .

Success may emasculate you if you let success go to your head. It emasculates you of your morality. That can happen if you're not a strong
person. And sad to say, most people aren't that strong. People allow
success to turn them. They start believing that they are as intelligent
and as omnipotent as their newfound "friends" tell them they are. Success didn't emasculate Gene.

ROBERT H. JUSTMAN

.　●　.

"Yes, but you know," I argue, "people who have been successful often end up with a lot of—stuff. Material wealth,
and servants, and so on, which make life easier. And then
they become less tolerant of anything that is not what they
want to do, when they want to do it. Or having what they
want, when they want it. You can see it. It shows on their
faces. That self-absorption. How does that improve the inner
man?"

"You think that you drive down a typical street in a typical
middle-class neighborhood and you don't see the same
faces?"

"I don't know. I live in a wealthy neighborhood. I'm concerned sometimes about what I see."

"I think I do know. I think in the best of all possible
worlds—in the world I dream of, in Star Trek—it is a better
world because it is a wealthier world. You don't have any
needs to drive you into bitterness. There's plenty of food.
What one is concerned with is not food and physical success;
one is concerned with happiness. And there is less and less
unhappiness in the world that I visualize because it's a
wealthier world. You don't have people saying, 'God, it's terrible, because I've never had a chance, you know, I've never

really had a chance.' And, oh boy, that can create terrible bitterness. You don't have those people in the Star Trek world I dream about. You don't have people chasing unrealized dreams. And that's what makes you bitter, and disappointed, and makes you choose false dreams. In the Star Trek future, people don't choose false dreams because the whole canopy of excitement and self-realization is always there."

He is not addressing current reality, something I have come to expect—and something for which, I feel, certain future generations will thank him. To him there is no point in looking at a problem in one time dimension. He believes in the future: it is here, adjacent to—or perhaps intrinsic to—the present. It is his extraordinary ability to ignore time that gives rise to his vision.

"There is no money in Star Trek," I remark. "Money doesn't even exist."

"No. Money is a terrible thing. Why do people work at jobs in Star Trek? Why does someone become a baker? Because the family is going to starve to death? No. People become bakers because certain people love the smell of things baking, and certain people take pride—we all have a little pride—in something. 'Let me give this to you because it's delicious and you will love it.' "

" 'And I made it.' "

" 'And I made it, yes! And this is my recipe.' " He looks into his mind for a moment. "All things will be taken care of."

He has an odd way of speaking today—like a prophet, a parent, and a cosmic administrator all at the same time.

"For example, I was looking for someone's father," he says, not bothering to tell me he was looking in his head. He knows I know, by this time. "And he was a very wise man and he had spent much of his life out in space, contemplating these things. And what this father had decided to do was adopt a square mile of forest and work in that square mile, and make it better. Fertilize things, prune saplings, and make everything in that square mile the best possible thing. God, that would be—wouldn't that be a wonderful way to live?" He looks at me with shining eyes.

"Yes, especially if you were feeling it all the time."

"Well, you probably would if it were a thing you wanted to feel. So you see, the need to work should not be a financial need, particularly when we are part of a better world. It is true. I haven't worked for money in the last twenty years. I've done good work because it's necessary for me to do good work. My pride. I couldn't write a bad script if I tried. I have to write good scripts because I like things working out properly. I happen to be one who likes scripts to be lovely and pleasant and spell a little message that says to you and my son—and a thousand other people—'It's best that you do something good.' That's my way. And it pays rich dividends, but never a dividend that I have worked for."

"No," I say, feeling a sudden surge of affection for this simple, complex, happily contradictory man. "No. You have to do what you love."

.　●　.

"So, what do you think of me so far?" He leans back and smiles.

"That you are a very religious person," I say, to see what will happen.

His face is worth a thousand words. "You can't possibly think that."

"Oh, but I do."

The Conversation

He thinks of arguing. I can see it rise in his face. He changes his mind. "Why?" he asks, very politely.

"Will you accept the definition of religion simply as ideology, just for the moment?"

"Only because I love you."

"Then I think that you are immersed in an ideology called Star Trek; that you adhere or try to adhere strictly to its precepts, even as they change, or you change them; that its epistemology is enlightenment—or evolution, if you prefer—and that you have your own personal Trinity: Humanity, Wife, and Holy Ghost."

"Who's the Holy Ghost?" he asks.

I give him a look.

"Spock," we both say together.

.   •   .

"I dislike the word 'holy,' " he says, "but there is a certain attitude I have towards Spock: I hold him in a kind of awe. His intelligence, his mastery over the problem-solving process. I think I would disagree with your terms, if only because they represent historical definitions, but I can accept their meaning. You may well be right. I don't know. I'll have to think about that one. Spock has for me so much significance, such personal and impersonal appeal. My Spock—not the one you see in *Star Trek*—although they are similar."

"What's the impersonal appeal?"

"Just that. Impersonal."

"I don't understand."

"Well, I don't know that I do either. It's a way he has of being detached but not deficient. He has a coldness to him that I admire."

"Why do you admire coldness?"

The Conversation

"Perhaps that's a bad description. I mean he has the ability to focus on a thing with such intensity that he freezes out distractions. But he remains intact. Spock is an intact entity: he dismisses extraneous concerns when he is involved in problem solving. He removes himself and even his great intellect so that his inner wisdom takes over. He can belong to the present moment, in a way that I never can. Majel has that ability. She can focus. She lives entirely in the present. It's a great asset, at times. A great asset. I don't know what it is about Spock that enables him to do that so well. It's something I have to make an effort to achieve."

"Maybe he is more limited than you. You always see so many sides of everything."

"Maybe. Maybe, too, he has that ability you have of cutting through the crap. I don't know. I call it a kind of coldness. I love it. It leaves me free. A very positive trait."

.   .   .

Within a few months, both Majel and I will have each been called cold. I note the circumstances, remember this conversation, do not mention it, and take the accusation as a compliment. Majel ignores it. Once it has been said, the present is past. She has no interest in it.

.   .   .

"You know what I think?" I say to Gene, one morning at breakfast.

"No," he says. "But I'm always glad to find out."

"Something that Isaac Asimov created in *The Naked Sun,* about 'viewing' versus 'seeing.' "

"Refresh my memory."

"The people called Solarians, one of the fifty outerworlds that humans had colonized many years before, created a culture in which they were entirely dependent on robots, and their estates were so large that they rarely had contact with anyone—neighbors, friends. Eventually, they evolved a culture in which each adult lived alone, surrounded by robots, and communicated with others only by viewing, a kind of holographic visiting called trimensional viewing."

"Oh yes," he says, "I may have borrowed that holographic idea from Isaac. I don't remember."

"Well, even though this holograph was a simultaneous, present transmission—that is, not a tape—they never considered themselves to be 'seen' by another person. So if they were having a bath, or doing any other private activity—not sex, because they couldn't stand human contact—they would visit with you via holograph. But they would never dream of being seen in that state. They felt that the projection of themselves was not the same as themselves. And I wonder, sometimes, if that isn't what you do. You project yourself, and it is yourself, but it's not the same as really seeing you."

"Well, but you would know that only because you see me. If you didn't, you wouldn't know the difference."

"Is there a difference?"

"Of course."

"So . . ."

"So those who can, see. Those who can't, view."

.   •   ·

"I'm sorry that I have never had a homosexual relationship," he remarks pensively, out of the blue, one afternoon.

The Conversation

"Because I know that there must be many joys and pleasures
and degrees of closeness in those relationships. I think that I
have in a way been cursed by having picked my particular
time period and background and so on, because I have no
doubt that I am capable of homosexualism."

"Do you think everyone is? Bisexual, I mean?"

"Oh yes. But you are a piece of your particular world, and
the different strengths of emotions that formed you and so
on. The things you were taught to regard as correct. But I am
very pleased with the fact that I have come out of that way of
thinking, in my time. As a matter of fact, remind me—I'm in
the midst of making a decision about homosexuality, male
and female, and how we are going to treat it on *Star Trek,* the
lovely ways in which we will treat it, without defying present
average conventions."

"Remind you what?"

"To mention that I am presently thinking very deeply
about that."

. . .

By this I assume that this will be subject for a later conversation, when he has made his decision. It never is. His hour of
death is approaching.

. . .

I am interested in his having said he picked his time and
place, as if he remembered an existence before existence. I
ask him if he believes in reincarnation. He says no, but he
amends this statement later, asks me to substitute the words
"I don't know." I think back to a conversation we had once

when he was very tired. To hear the voice that speaks from its electronic repository now is to hear something hovering in the back of the primal consciousness—prophetic and haunting. Some people insist that he did not know he was dying. He did.

"What defeats you?" I had asked him. It was just next on the list of questions and had no particular significance until he answered it.

"I think the same thing that defeats you from time to time: you just can't . . . stay ahead of . . . humanity. You can't stay ahead of these characters." His voice, which would be strong tomorrow, was fragile, ephemeral, old. "You just . . ." He paused for a long time. "You have to occasionally say, 'I give up on that . . . I need a—I need to *rest*. I need to rethink the universe for a while. And, and then I think that having acknowledged the fact that you're human, and a part of all this—the fact *it* has the knowledge that does defeat you from time to time—then God, or whatever it is, somehow allows you to back up. Maybe take a fresh run at it. I, I'm just defeated by the fact that there are not enough thoughts in this vessel to really work it all out."

.   •   .

I wish I had learned more of humankind—of your own concept of your creator. I have seen much to criticize in mankind. But I believe there's even more to admire. Had I more time, I might have learned to understand humanity's greatest of all achievements: the ability to feel love for one another.

QUESTOR, *THE QUESTOR TAPES*

.   •   .

The Conversation

We speak of love once. It arises out of silence one morning when he is not feeling well. He is tired. His eyes register
pain. I stop asking questions, and in unspoken agreement we
sit in his study, wordless: I, on the floor, writing, he dozing
lightly in his chair. Once or twice, he looks down with an
apologetic smile. When I have finished my notes, he is deeply
asleep. I rest my head on the arm of his chair, and later awake
to find his hand on my cheek.

"I'm feeling better," he says politely and untruthfully.
"What shall we talk about?"

I look up into a face from which the life is draining daily,
and can think of only one thing. "How about love?"

"Sounds good," he replies. "I'll just collect my thoughts.
What do you think about it?"

"I think that you do not want to be loved."

"That's nonsense," he says, startled and somewhat pleased
at this new challenge. "What makes you say that?"

"It's true, isn't it?"

"Of course it's not true. I *love* love."

"But you love loving. You don't much care for being
loved."

"I don't see how you can say that," he answers, with a
laugh. "You know me better than that."

While I am thinking of how to explain what I mean, he
frowns. "You're not giving me that 'fear of intimacy' shit, are
you? Because if you are, I've heard it before."

"No. I'm giving you some Saint Francis shit."

"Saint Francis? Now what are you talking about?" He sits
up straighter, ready for battle.

"Your approach to life, your philosophy, *you*, remind me of
Saint Francis of Assisi."

His face is a perfect portrait of consternation. "I never

The Conversation

know what you're going to say next," he says. "How can I remind you of a saint, in the first place? And, in the second place, you may know me, but you don't know him. Or," he adds with a laugh, "do you?"

"Sort of. I was a Franciscan."

"Oh, well," he says, thinking this one over. "Well, well, go on."

"There is a prayer, call it a yearning, attributed to Saint Francis. I'll say it to you. Just to avoid argument, I'll leave out the references to the disputed deity, and while I'm saying it, you think of Starfleet, Captain Kirk, the Prime Directive, and Gene Roddenberry, okay?"

"Okay," he says, settling back and preparing to be amused.

I begin. As I recite it, his face changes. His thumb begins to rotate.

"Make me an instrument of peace.
Where there is hatred, let me sow love;
Where there is injury, pardon;
Where there is doubt, faith;
Where there is despair, hope;
Where there is darkness, light;
And where there is sadness, joy.
"Grant that I may not so much seek
To be consoled as to console;
To be understood as to understand;
To be loved, as to love.
"There's more," I tell him, "but that's the relevant part."

He lets out a long breath, says nothing for a time. Finally, he shakes his head slowly. "That's very beautiful," he says in a quiet voice. "Is that how you think of me—an instrument of peace?"

"I think a lot of people think of you—and Star Trek—like that."

The Conversation

"Oh, I would love that. I hope I am, in some small way, an instrument of peace." He sighs, reaches down, and kisses the top of my head. "I'm so happy to know you," he says.

"And, you see, the part about being loved, Gene—just from knowing you these few months, it seems to me that it is a matter of focus. Your purpose, or mission, or job—you say it yourself—is to love humanity. Being loved is secondary. At least, being loved in the traditional sense. It strikes me that you love humanity not because it is made up of individuals whom you cherish, but, rather, you love individuals because they are representatives of humanity, the whole socio-organism. And so, love in its ordinary one-on-one manifestation, in which you love and are loved, just isn't that important. Maybe because being an instrument of peace is more important. Helping people love each other."

"I never would have thought about it like that," he says, "but I have to say you're right." He looks at me strangely. "How do you know this?"

"I don't know that I do. It's just a thought."

"Well, with that thought, I think you have hit the core of Gene Roddenberry. And Star Trek, as you said. I really do. I'm going to do some pretty hard thinking about it. We weren't really playing our game, but this time, you found me." He shakes his head again. "You found me, all right."

. • .

We return to the subject of controversial topics for *Star Trek*.

"Writing is really at the heart of it all," he says. "Everything depends on a good script. Some of the things we were talking about are awaiting a good script. Of course, they're awaiting something even more important: a certain readiness on the part of the audience. I have to be careful, not so much with what I decide to put on a particular show, but how I treat it. I could do a show about homosexuality, for example, and have half the viewers cheering me on. Well, in the case of our audience, not half. I hope we have a greater percentage of enlightenment than that, in our fans. But to do a pro-gay episode—or any other controversial issue—you have to do this." He holds up his thumb and finger spaced about a half inch apart.

"A little at a time?"

"A little at a time. People have to get used to these things. They have to get used to a certain liberation of thought, in the same manner as captive animals need to get used to freedom when you let them out of their cages. Suddenly they've got to survive in a world of options. Nobody's going to feed them. Nobody's going to tell them that this or that option is bad or good. They'll have to try different things, and see if something works. And if it doesn't, what should they do next? Oh yes, a whole world opens up."

"Meanwhile dealing with all the others who have opted not to leave the cage," I say. "Don't forget them. The peer-pressure lot."

"The first duty is to get away from them as soon as possible. You can come back later, when you've gained a little confidence and maturity and say, 'Look—here—this is what I've found.' I think the best stories in drama have been about this kind of unappreciated enlightenment. But let's look at these few adventurers who've gone into strange new worlds. They have their own cage philosophy inside them—they've got to fight that too. Humans are so wonderful, so brave. It's astonishing, the way the human spirit has survived. There are

so many shows I would like to create based on variations of
this theme."

"But you're not still actively engaged in producing *Next Gen*."

"Not as active as I once was. My people are all good people, Rick Berman in particular. I trust him to produce *my* show. And he does. But I still look at everything. I make my evaluations and put my stamp of approval on everything. Nothing goes on that I don't approve."

I know this, of course. In the many weeks of our unfolding relationship, we have gone over scripts together, watched dailies together, discussed the relative merits of one word over another in line changes. He has sent me over to the set of *Star Trek VI: The Undiscovered Country,* where I have watched the legendary Kirk and Spock in action. We have discussed that legend and how it affected the production of *The Next Generation,* and I have heard him on the phone with a great number of staff with regard to the show. Watching dailies is so different from watching the finished product, with commercial interruptions, that a thought arises.

"Do you ever watch *Star Trek* on TV?" I ask.

"Oh yes. Sometimes with a sense of wonder." He shakes his head in obvious delight. "It's twenty-five years old!" he says, as if it were a new thought. He is speaking here of the phenomenon of Star Trek and is clearly in awe of his own creation.

"I'd like to watch it with you," I tell him. "It would be like a triple time shift: creator and created; progenitor and descendent; subject, object, and observer. *Star Trek* or *Next Gen,* or both."

"Let's do that," he says enthusiastically. "I'd like to do that. Yes, and we can comment."

・ ● ・

We do. But we do not comment. It is weeks later. He is in the hospital. They have attached him to wires, bored holes in his head. Injected, medicated, monitored him. Now they come in to test him. A team of doctors ask him questions to determine the state of his—logical capacity, memory, brain functions? I don't know. They ask him the date, the year, to count this and answer that. He makes a few mistakes. When they leave, he says to me, "Time?" I say, "A couple of minutes after seven." He looks at the television in his room and says, *"Star Trek."* I turn it on. The *Enterprise* sails across the screen. Whatever else he forgets in the last days of his life, this is not one. Nor is his critical ability impaired in that world. Once, one of the characters says something he does not like. "No," he says. I do not speak. He is working.

・ ● ・

He wants to talk about actors, now, the medium of his dream: what they represent; how they convey meaning; what happens to the written word when it becomes the spoken; the difference between good acting and good performance. Three-dimensional entertainment. He asks me so many questions that it is difficult to ask my own. When I do, he replies candidly, then asks me not to repeat most of it. I erase the tape, make a few notes, and ask his permission to include the following. He agrees.

"I want to tell you something," he says, conspiratorially. "I share something very fundamental with actors."

"Oh?"

"Yes. It's a kind of belief. When they get up there and pre-

tend to be or take on a certain character, they have such a
belief—the good ones—that that character exists. I'm like
that. I like to believe in that, and I'm amazed that it still happens, because I created all this, and I see what's behind it all,
and it still works. I can be moved, like the audience. I love
that."

"You can still be the audience?"

"Yes, isn't it wonderful? I'm still the audience. And, as the
audience, yourself," he says, leaning forward with interest,
"tell me what good acting means to you."

"I suppose when the actor disappears, and the character
takes over."

"Yes, I think that's largely true. It's a noble ideal. But then,
of course, when they achieve it, they complain that they're
typecast and wallow in misery about it." He searches his conscience for a moment. "Some of them," he adds.

I ask him who. He tells me. We go on.

"Who disappears to you in *Star Trek*?" he asks.

"Oh, Leonard, of course. He really becomes Spock."

Gene starts to speak. I interrupt him. "I know you are
Spock, but you aren't the manifestation of Spock. Leonard's
face—his fingers, the way he breathes in, in distress—that is
the corporeal Spock. Leonard does tend to disappear. Ask
anyone to show you a picture of Spock, they'll show you
Leonard Nimoy's face."

He is quiet for a while. "He really did do a wonderful job,
didn't he?" he says in paternal acknowledgment. "I was—I
am very proud of him. I wonder how much of the internal
Spock he has left in him."

.   •   .

The Conversation

When I meet Leonard Nimoy a few months later, I search for signs of Spock in his face. They are there. Whatever else is there, he keeps hidden. He will not talk to me.

．　●　．

"Who else?" Gene asks, coming back from a personal trip into the past. "Who else disappears?"

"Oh, all of them, I suppose. Leonard, consistently. Patrick Stewart, certainly. I don't know; I am the worst person to judge."

"Surely not. One of the best, I would say."

"But I'm not a representative viewer," I tell him. "I often watch television and movies for very bad reasons. Or rather very good reasons of my own. Bad as a judge for your purposes."

He, of course, becomes more interested. "Tell me anyway."

"Okay, we're going to have an argument, I can tell. But to me the words often mean more than anything. Not just their meaning, although that is most important, but their sound. I would watch *Star Trek* if Patrick Stewart read all the parts. Or Brent. Or any of the principals, really, to see what shape they took, what meaning they had, when coming out of different mouths."

"Oh yes," he says, "but you wouldn't watch it every week. After that particular approach had been explored—and it might be a very interesting thing to explore—you'd look for something else. You'd return to our format, because it is more complex, and that is what makes it consistently interesting."

"No doubt. But I think it's amazing how form changes content, depending on the actor. When you find one whose suspension of self allows the script to come through, for that particular character, then you watch it for the acting as well as the words."

"So far I can't argue with that. Would you like to be a casting director?"

"No. Because, to me, if you have a really good script, then I'd watch it. Whether any of the actors disappeared or not. The script takes over sometimes."

"Bad acting can ruin a script. People won't watch that."

"I will."

He shakes his head. "No you wouldn't."

"I told you, I'm the wrong person to ask."

"Perhaps you shouldn't be a casting director."

"Oh, I *know* if it's good acting or not. I just don't care sometimes. It's the words, you see."

"What do you mean?" he says. "Words speak louder than acting?"

"Yes, sometimes they do. When they are saying something. At other times, they don't matter at all."

"When don't they?"

"Oh, well, for that matter if it were announced that Charlton Heston were going to recite his grocery list on television at six o'clock this evening, I'd tape it."

Gene leans back and roars with laughter. "Heston? Oh, you wouldn't have to do that. He's a friend of Majel's. She can call him up and maybe he'll come down and read our grocery list to you." He chuckles. "I'm dying to know your reasons for this one." I look at him sharply.

"I'm serious. I really am," he says. "We may be getting to some fundamental ideas about acting that I want to explore."

"It has very little to do with acting. It might be the flick of of an eyelid, a cheekbone, a mesmerizing inflection, the ability to cry copiously and silently, with grace. Bits. Not the whole performance. I might watch a movie for two hours to see someone blow out a match. As far as Mr. Heston goes, I can't know if he is a good actor or not. He is bound up with a transitional moment in my life: he is a ten-year-old's version of the heroic ideal versus the fallible, and the inevitable. I thought he was *the* perfect actor then. I preserve that in myself. I refuse to judge. No. I would listen to the grocery list because of the perfect moment, the second—the nanosecond in which, perhaps 'a sack of dog food' because of the timbre of his voice, becomes present. The dog food is there. I see it."

"And you don't think that is good acting?"

"It is a good performance. It is a miraculous performance if the dog food materializes, spills from its blue sack on the wet tiled floor."

"You're talking about radio, not television."

"No I'm not."

"Well . . ." He struggles between objection and curiosity. Curiosity wins. "What if it doesn't?"

"Doesn't what?"

"Doesn't materialize—you don't *see* the dog food."

"Then I just trip out on his nose. He has a perfect nose."

"Somehow, I don't think that means what it would mean if someone else said it. Why don't you tell me a little more about it."

"No. You're supposed to be doing the talking."

"Oh, I'll have plenty to say in a minute. You go on."

"Well, that's exactly why I *am* talking about television. I think actors—or to be precise, visible actors—are objects, in a sense. They have, or should have, no substance of their own. No content. They should be conduits of content, of the script. They should disappear. Their characters should inhabit them. But if they don't, or don't entirely, or don't always, then one can invest them with one's own content. Or they can provide simple visual pleasure: they can be a springboard for, I don't know, musing perhaps. Heston's nose in that case takes on the same meaning as a Caravaggio—a Vermeer nose. It becomes representational. We move, I move, from the expectation of infusion to one of perception. He—all actors are like paintings or sculptures—it is up to them to become their own Pygmalions and burst into life. And if, for some reason, they don't or can't, then there is always the delightful possibility of the principle of Heston's nose. Representational reality."

"I've always said that television is art. I absolutely agree with you on that. And it goes back to one of the earliest principles of theater. Greek theater set out to achieve that interrelationship between the visual and verbal. It's a very pure form of entertainment, isn't it? Very sparse and beautiful."

"Oh yes, people wailing in tragedy with grapes hanging off their heads."

He laughs again. "So you invest a performance with your own imagination?"

"If it allows that."

"You might like to be a producer. A producer has a very special relationship with the audience. He has to see a performance from both sides of the screen, something a writer can't always do. We get marvelous scripts sometimes, but they just won't work for television. I'm always sorry about that."

"Can't you make them work?"

"Not usually, in those instances. Usually, we just have to take the idea and dispense with some very wonderful writing

The Conversation

that would be better off in a book. That's something I've learned from experience. I've never found out why. I just know it. It's just television. I want to go back to your caveat. You said you often watch something for bad reasons—or good reasons—of your own. When you watch something at other times, for its own merits as a production, what sorts of things would they be?"

"Talking heads. *Masterpiece Theater* sometimes. *Star Trek* and *Next Gen,* the Road Runner—"

"The cartoon?"

"Yes."

"Why?"

"Timing, I think. It's a masterpiece of timing. The Road Runner always says 'Beep beep' about two seconds after you expect him to. It's great comedy. Or, at least I think it's funny."

"Oh yes, timing is very important. In humor and in drama. How interesting. What else?"

"Mostly British productions. No offense, but I think, in general, British TV is superior to American TV. Most of what I watch is PBS stuff. But I also watch American TV—actually, reruns sometimes. I don't have a lot of time, but when I do I watch *Dragnet,* because—I don't know why really. It's campy."

"I used to write for *Dragnet.* How lovely to hear that you watch it."

"Yes, I know. It reminds me of *Star Trek,* the original series, sometimes."

"In what way?"

"It has a similar earnestness. Its comments on society are almost a plea to humanity. I don't know—maybe it's all that orange paint and plastic plants. I don't have a profound rea-

son. I just like it. Recognizing it for what it is. It's not Ten-
nessee Williams. Why are you asking all the questions?"

"I'm coming to a point. Now tell me what it is that moti-
vates you to turn on the television, to watch something for its
wholeness rather than its parts. And afterward, to say, 'That
was a good show.' Or even, 'a great show'?"

"Forgetfulness."

"What?"

"I forget that I am there. I forget to think my thoughts; I
think the thoughts of those characters on the screen. I guess I
forget that I am a separate person. I guess it all adds up to
representation of self. I am no longer an observer—I am
those characters, they are me."

"Yes. Character. Exactly. And that is art. In *Star Trek* we try
not just to make you see the dog food—although that is a
wonderful thing, a wonderful thing to be able to do, especially for an audience such as you, who would want to create
images of her own. But in *Star Trek* we want you to be the
one reciting that list of groceries, to see how it feels to say 'a
box of dog food' yourself. And that's why I say television is
art. Some people may think that is a silly thing to say, but I
believe it."

"Why?"

"I'll tell you why, in a minute. But first, let me tell you why
I disagree with you, on two points you made. First of all, an
actor has to keep some of his own content—he really does.
That's what makes one actor differ from another. Maybe
what you mean is that he has to get rid of a certain amount of
ego, in the Jungian sense. In most cases, a great amount of
ego."

"Actually, I didn't mean that. I meant what I said. So you
can feel quite comfortable in denouncing it. And anyway, I

The Conversation

know you're going to make me change my mind. Besides, you're the producer of the most-beloved, most-watched show on television. I really have no right to disagree with you on this subject at all."

"Oh no, no, no. I am the producer of the most-watched and most-beloved show on television for only one reason. Because there's an audience out there—there are fans. I try to tell my people this constantly—the actors especially. God, I wish it wasn't so hard to get this through their heads. They can turn out the most magnificent performance ever filmed, and if there's no one there, it means nothing. Drama is story-telling, communicating between people. If there is no audience to communicate with, there is no show, period. We owe our existence to the viewers."

"If there is no show, or if it is an inadequate show, there is no audience."

"Yes, of course, that's a given. I am so convinced of the excellence of our series, that I wouldn't think to mention that. But it's a symbiotic relationship: there is equal value in each. Equal. You must respect the audience. Many of them are more intelligent than the actors and actresses they watch. Try and tell an actor or actress that. I'm not talking about our people here—they're all very good, they've learned that, or are learning it. I think the fact that they have to go to conventions—to meet the people who are responsible for their jobs—keeps them aware of why they're up there. But my point is that you have every right to discuss your experience as a viewer with any producer in the world. And not just you, but anyone. In fact, I would call it an obligation. There would be a lot less crap on American television today if more producers spent more time talking with the people they're trying to reach. A lot less crap.

The Conversation

"In our show, well, our fans feel rather proprietary about it. More the first show than our current series. As they should. They saved it, in the third season. And still today, they feel an obligation to respond to what we put out there in front of them every week. And that's good. That's a wonderful thing. I don't let the fans run my show. I run my show. But, boy, do I listen. And I'm really not disagreeing with you, personally. You have very unique reasons for the way you perceive things—more of a creator's take. But an average television audience doesn't look at a show in this poetic way. So let me address you now as that representative audience you spoke of.

"Going back to that ego thing . . . I think you were closer to the truth when you said, 'a suspension of self.' An actor has to suspend his or her ego in order to let the character get through—not obliterate himself. It's an intermix. 'Suspension' is a good word. A really good actor coexists with his character: he has a personal relationship with him, and he bows out graciously to let the character shine. Actors have to feel what the character feels—I'm sure this isn't news to you—but they have to keep just enough ego to turn in a real, human, believable performance. They can't be watching themselves act, like so many bad actors do—in that sense, they have to disappear, yes. But they have to disappear to themselves, not to the audience. Not completely—or else it's no different from having robots playing the part of humans."

"That would be interesting. I'd love to see that."

"Oh no, that would be, that would be . . . It *would* be interesting, wouldn't it?" He stops for a moment, riveted by this idea. "Maybe that's the way it is in the future. And actors are those who control the robots' movements and program their voices."

The Conversation

"Yes, a thespian renaissance. A company of Datas, doing Shakespeare. Except that Data is an android, not a robot. What's the difference anyway?"

He is still contemplating mechanical actors brought to life by their human counterparts, in some distant segment of time. "What?" he asks. "Oh, I don't know, exactly. I don't remember. Actually I do know, but I've forgotten for the moment. You might ask Brent tomorrow. I'm taking you to the studio. I want you to spend time on the set, to see for yourself what it takes to bring my Star Trek to life." He returns to the idea of robots. "There is a technology out there that is working on that very possibility."

We get sidetracked on what is now called virtual reality. When that discussion ends, I have to play back the tape to find out where we were.

"You said you disagreed with me on two points," I say. "What's the second?"

"Your reference to Pygmalion—that actors should become their own Pygmalions, bring themselves to life. That is true, but it's a role they share with the director. A good director gets into the characters—from a different standpoint. He draws out that life. You'll see that tomorrow. And I think that largely happens on our show. We have excellent directors; all our people are first-class. And now I'm going to tell you a little secret: I *like* our people."

"That's no secret."

"Oh, it is," he says. "Because some folks out there may think that I have said it in the past to be supportive, or to convey some wonderful impression. The secret part is that it's the truth. I want you to say that for me. This is strictly 'for the record.' I'm genuinely very happy with the cast we have now, and I think that they are happy with each other."

He goes on to tell me various stories about the strengths,
weaknesses, vulnerabilities, talents he has observed in each of
"his people." He discusses their early interviews, their development into the characters they portray, his perception of
them as people and as performers. It is strictly off the record,
but when he concludes, I ask permission to quote his last
sentence. He gives it: "They are all beloved to me."

· ● ·

When we are discussing the former conversation—edit-
ing specific examples, deleting extraneous asides—we begin
to talk about acting again. Something immediately comes to
mind that I am hesitant to say.

"Go on, say it," Gene says. "I think I know what you're
thinking."

"Well . . . *Star Trek,* the original series."

"What about it?"

"Look, I love that show. That's why I'm here. I found
something in it that said 'Gene Roddenberry,' something that
urged me to go to the source of all those ideas. But . . ."

"It isn't always well acted? Is that what you're so reluctant
to say? Don't be. It isn't going to hurt my feelings."

"Well, I don't know if it is or isn't. That's the problem. But
that's also the point. It just doesn't matter. And in fact, I think
if it had been more polished, more subtle, then it wouldn't
have had the impact it did."

"Well, why would you say that? There is so much I would
improve on if I were doing it again. Not just acting, but, so
many things. As I have done in *The Next Generation.* You're
not speaking of that series are you?"

"No. I think what I mean is that the original series was

more representational, more like classic mythology, with an idealism expressed in a representative way. Kirk, hero, period. Spock, logic, period. Like Superman or Flash Gordon or Roy Rogers. I look at them more as figures of qualities: courage, compassion, et cetera. Personifications of the ideal."

"Like Greek theater?"

"Maybe. Maybe that's why I love it. Or maybe it's that Heston thing. I refuse to judge. And please don't think I am disparaging the cast, because I'm not. I don't think that an Academy Award performance is the point."

"Emmy," he says. "It's a television show. But alright, that may be part of the reason it had and continues to have such appeal. Perhaps the acting suits the purpose in a way you don't realize. Because you come away with a perfect sense of character, don't you? You know who Kirk is and Uhura and all of them. You could tell me right now what Sulu would do and what he wouldn't. You have a sense of them as people."

"Absolutely. An absolute sense. Perhaps it is perfect acting. I don't know. I know that I watch it and that I feel great affection for the characters. They are who they are completely, but they're not really anybody I might meet on the street."

"No, but they might be people you might like to meet on the street. I think I understand you, but I would take exception to your notion that acting consists only of the kinds of performances given in *Masterpiece Theater*. Other kinds of acting are just as valid. I think that's your problem. You're looking for a kind of great drama in a television show that was designed to sell a product—to keep many millions of people buying that product. PBS shows don't have to do that. And, as I told you, I am thinking of doing a series that could easily fit that bill. But I understand—and I think we have come to

a different way of expressing ideas in *The Next Generation*. It
is more subtle, as you point out. We have more money and
more time and more freedom to create something that is
more of what we expect today. We don't need to hammer
people over the head with messages. They're there, alright,
but I think we get them across in much better ways: We incorporate more qualities within each character, so that you
don't have Picard, hero, period. They all have their heroic
qualities and their failings. They are all less of a caricature of
a particular quality. And they all have room to improve, in a
believable, down-to-earth way. So much of my philosophy
hinges on improvement, on evolution. We continue to evolve
in the Star Trek world."

"I don't want to go on record as saying that the acting is
bad in *Star Trek*. I don't mean that."

"You don't have to go on record as saying anything you
don't want to."

"But this is an important point. The show is unprecedented
in the history of television. It has spawned a subculture that is
rapidly becoming part of mainstream culture. With its weird
sets and rubbery aliens, and a sort of larger-than-life method
of acting—why does it survive?"

"It survives, I think, because it fills a need," he says slowly.
"We need that larger-than-life experience. You see, you
wouldn't love it if the acting wasn't exactly what it is: an
identification with these very strong characters. And if the
characters were larger than life, then that's what the actors
had to do—show that."

"Yes, and it was twenty-five years ago. All television was
different, younger then. Which is why, I guess, you often
refer to the two *Star Trek* shows as 'the growing up of Gene
Roddenberry.' I'm not questioning why we loved it then. It's

more a question of why it is equally or even more beloved now, in the '90s. Even though *Next Gen* is so extraordinarily successful, people still watch the original series."

"Possibly because it is the '90s. This isn't a very happy time for humanity. And in *Star Trek,* both of them, my dreams speak to the inner wish of humanity to be happy—to live in a world where such people might exist. People of courage, people who can disagree with one another and not let their disagreements erupt into war, who can simply say, 'I will not interfere with your way of life, and thank you for not interfering with mine.' To be a part of the Star Trek dream means to be the sort of person who does not have to depend on others for self-worth or self-definition—who have been given the chance by the very world they are living in to seek their own answers. Not to be afraid of that. The original cast got that message across very well. Boy, did they get that message across. And continue to."

.   •   .

I am curious about why he wanted to spend so much time talking about acting—insisted that the conversations above be included in a portrait of his mind. His answer to that is that television is dangerous. "It is the most dangerous force in the world today."

.   •   .

Literate humans have known for dozens of centuries that people's opinions and values are affected by what they see, and that dramatic portrayals of life are often much stronger than the reality around people . . . this is what literature is all about, whether it is carried in the printed word or on stage or in a comic book or on an electric tube. Drama, and particularly fictional drama, has always had enormous effects on the audience—much more than facts or news usually do—because the essence of drama is to take the audience and force them to become part of the story, to identify with the participants, and to feel as they feel, and often to think as they think. So there is no question that what people see on television affects them, but this very fact opens up a whole spectrum of subjects that are usually ignored. . . . For example, did the juvenile commit violence because he saw a similar version portrayed on the screen, or was it because his attitudes and values had already been twisted and eroded by all of the television he had been watching for years? This is where the simplistic cause-and-effect arguments break down. How could you blame a robbery dramatization on one show, and ignore the damage caused by years of anesthetizing the juvenile's brain with inane kiddy shows, the vulgar materialism of game shows, where he is seeing adults prostituting themselves into jackasses to win a new car; and the snake-oil commercials, in which even a child can see the inherent deceit?

CONGRESSIONAL RECORD STATEMENT OF GENE RODDENBERRY

.   •   .

"You see," he says, "I would really prefer to do a show that would not have to rely on advertising to appear on television. I'd like to do a series along the lines that you mentioned— that would have a much smaller audience. But that would be irresponsible of me, because I have ideas that I know are right for our time, and they have to reach the greatest number of people possible. And that, for now, means commercial television. It is a restriction, but it is one I willingly accept because of the benefits. I may lose something as a creator, as a writer, but it is nothing compared to what millions would lose if we didn't have a Star Trek to dream about."

There is a look on his face that I have come to recognize. It is remote, determined, austere. A Spock look.

"There is a future," he says, with the emphasis on *is,* "and it is because of people like Kirk and Picard and so on—people who recognize that the future is a personal responsibility."

"Like you."

"Yes. I have to do what I can. And television is the way I can do it. That's why the actors and the acting are so important. Don't mistake me—it is a team effort. No one is more important than anyone else. The supervising producers, the editors, the makeup—Michael Westmore does an incredible job—I want you to see everything: special effects, wardrobe, everything. We'll do that. I want you to be part of this. And when you've seen everything, I want you to tell me, from everything we've said, everything we've talked about, how much you see of my Star Trek dreamworld in my *Star Trek* television show. But—and here's a big *but*—the actors are what the public sees. When Picard makes a wonderful, thrilling statement, the audience will say, Picard is a man who believes in this or that—isn't he marvelous—isn't he intelligent? And maybe, 'I would like to be like that.' And they start thinking like that. And they begin to . . . to . . ."

"Embody some of the traits of the future?"

"Yes, exactly. The kind of future we need. They don't say, 'Wow—isn't that writer John Doe fabulous? What wonderful things he dreams of! I would like to be like that.' Oh no. It is the actors who carry the message. It's not fair, but that's the way it is. And that's why I try to choose people to whom this is not just a job. It's not always possible, but I think everyone feels in different degrees that what we are doing is valuable, that it means something. And that's why it hurts me when . . ." He launches into a discussion about Leonard Nimoy and William Shatner. He says nothing derogatory. It is simply a puzzle to him as to why there is an estrangement between them and Star Trek, meaning himself.

"The others have always been loyal to me, loyal to Star Trek," he continues. "Nichelle is wonderful. George and Jimmy and Walter are wonderful. I want you to meet them. You will find a very special quality in those people."

"You left out De Forrest Kelley."

"Oh, I didn't mean to. De's a friend. I would say a real one. Forgive me, De! You see, that's why I didn't like most of the movies. I wanted the other characters to be brought back strongly. I wanted to create what we finally created in Four [*Star Trek IV: The Voyage Home*]. The secondary actors remained loyal to me, loyal to the Star Trek ideal. I don't know what Six will be like. If I like it, I'll put my name on it. If I don't, I won't."

"May I quote you on this?"

"No. I don't want to hurt anyone. Write it up and read it to me on the phone. I'll let you know."

Above is the edited result.

"So you see," he goes on, "actors and acting are crucial to my purpose."

"The actors are helping to create a future, your vision of the future, by representing it on television. By making the present, future—and the future, present."

"Yes. If there were another, better way to do it, I would. I prefer books. In fact, I am writing a book right now. It's about what happens to Kirk after he retires from Starfleet. Who is he then? What does he become? But books just don't have the impact they used to, which I think is unfortunate. But I work with these misfortunes. I do what I have to."

"What is it, in one sentence, that you have to do? What is your Prime Directive?"

"In one sentence? Ensure that when the future arrives, there are still humans in it."

.   •   .

We who are in the television industry and take our responsibilities seriously often do not know whether to laugh or cry when family-hour censorship comes up, because it is censorship that created this unwanted violence everyone is talking about. We in the industry are not that barren of ideas . . . we are capable of fashioning an exciting drama out of the thousands of real issues of life and the rights and wrongs of conflicts which exist in everything: sex, religion, politics, corporate life, militarism, and everything else. The structure of television, however, does not allow our people often to write on these things, and when you take all the meaningful subjects away from a writer, all you have left is sex and violence with which to provide the conflict that is necessary to draw the mass audience. This is not because television networks are evil, or that their executives are thoughtless men. Like us, they work in a medium whose primary corporate purpose is really not to entertain, and not to inform, and this is something that is very seldom brought up when these subjects come up. Our basic problem is this is not the primary purpose of television. The primary purpose of television is to sell products. It is structured that way, not because of any diabolical plan, but because that is the way it happened to grow up. And these commercial messages demand mass audiences, and often this means the lower and lower-middle bulk audiences whose opinions are sufficiently malleable to be changed by commercial messages. I think even more unfortunately it is these same malleable minds which are most likely to be convinced that the meaning of life, the alpha and omega of existence, is in that breathtaking

vista somewhere between *The Beverly Hillbillies* and *Let's Make a Deal.*
We are no longer dealing with that pleasant little idiot-box gadget
which we can watch occasionally for entertainment and some shop-
ping information. We are dealing in television, gentlemen, with a
sound-and-image device of incredible potency, which is now being
used in this country at the astonishing rate of something like billions
of people hours each week. It begins to appear that our children are
watching television for two hours for every one hour actually spent
studying or reading books. And the adults probably come off with
much less. And to make this picture worse, our most respected engineers and scientists in this field tell us that the telecommunications
explosion is really just beginning. What we are probably dealing with
now, gentlemen, is nothing less than a wholly new form of human
communications, and it is something that may be as significant in its
own way, if you can believe this, as the invention of the Gutenberg
press, but we have no guarantee that the results of this are going to be
anywhere nearly as happy.

CONGRESSIONAL RECORD STATEMENT OF GENE RODDENBERRY

.   •   .

"So you see," he says simply. "I have to make *Star Trek*. I
just have to."

.   •   .

"Gene," I say one evening under the stars, "what is it that
makes you love humanity? Is it initiation or response?"
"What?"
"Well, so many people love you, or think they do, or love
parts of you, or love what you do, which is part of you, then
it would make it difficult for you not to respond similarly."

The Conversation

"Yes, but—I felt that way before it was a response."

We are quiet for a while.

"My mother tells a story," he says, "about dreaming of what she would do for all of her friends if she could—it was a wish—and it was to give all her friends gifts of the things they wanted most to have. I've heard that story several times, and I think it was something I was born with because of her."

"Have you been happy most of your life?"

"Yes. More the last part of my life. This is why I scolded you a little bit about success making people worse, because that is generally not true. The more success a person has, the better the hopes for that person."

"That's what Somerset Maugham says—that the idea that success spoils people by making them vain, egotistic, and self-complacent, is wrong. It is failure which makes people bitter and cruel."

"That must be why I loved Maugham from the first."

"And Mom," I say, wondering when I will meet her.

"And Mom," Gene says, smiling.

When I meet his mother, I feel a sense of recognition in this gentle, fragile lady. She is almost broken with grief over the death of her son, but speaks of him tearlessly. In the many visits and talks I have with her, she tells me stories and incidents of Gene's life. One thing brings him sharply to mind, and gives a reason for her quiet tearless sorrow. "I think of him all the time," she says. "I daydream about him."

· • ·

"The point of the writer," Somerset Maugham says in *The Summing Up*, "is that he is not one man, but many. It is because he is many that he can create many, and the measure of

his greatness is the number of selves that he comprises. . . .
His daydreams are so significant to him that it is the world of
sense that is shadowy, and he has to reach out for it with an
effort of will. His castles in Spain are no baseless fabric, but
real castles that he lives in."

When I read that passage, the last link in the chain of our
conversations forms, meets the first, clicks shut.

· • ·

"Do you remember," I ask Gene, "what you said on the
phone a while back—about your imagination, about nothing being real unless it exists in your dreamworld?"

"Yes, but not exactly. Play it back for me."

"I can't play it back. We were on the phone—I didn't tape
it. But I wrote it down." I read it to him: " '. . . nothing is
really real to me unless it also exists in my dreamworld.' "

"That's generally true," he says. "Why do you ask?"

"Majel."

"Oh," he says, looking toward the house. We are in the
garden. It is colder now.

"You daydream about her. She is part of your dreamworld.
You get angry when she is not perfect. She keeps the universe straight for you. She was your best friend, but now
Spock is, and yet you often speak of her as having the qualities Spock has: focus, living in the present, a kind of intimate
detachment. And you say you can't get into her dreamworld."

He looks around as though for a means of escape. His
thumb begins its customary cycle. "Well?" he asks after a
moment.

"Well, but that is what you want, isn't it? Your favorite

feeling is longing. You love longing—for the future, for elusive dreams, for answers, for her. That's where it all comes from, isn't it—this world you've created? It comes from longing, from not entirely possessing anything. Which, by the way, has a great deal in common with the monastic ideal. But that aside, there isn't really anything you want to . . . to have. Possess. Own. You just want it to be there, close enough so that you can long for it, far enough away that you can never reach it. And that's why reality doesn't really count unless it makes that leap fully, into your head—where you can re-create it."

He says nothing.

"She's a real person, Gene. You didn't create her. You asked me to explain her. I can't. All I know is that if you want to, you have to confront the living animal, not just a portrait mounted on the wall of your dreams. And if you think you can't get into her dreamworld, I'm surprised. You spend most of your life in it—her dreamworld is you."

He looks angry for a moment, and turns his face from me.

"I'm sorry if this is intrusive, I really am," I tell him. "But I didn't ask for this . . . this . . . assignment. You gave it to me. And that's my answer, for all it's worth."

He is silent for a long time.

"Give me a hug," he says finally, with his face still turned. When I do, he buries his face in my side.

"God, I love her," he says.

. • .

He has to believe in perfection. He has to. It is what he shares with those religions of the world he so despises, and the philosophers he has studied with meticulous care. It is

what he admires in his fictional heroes, what he created a
hunger for in millions who watch *Star Trek*, what propels him
toward the future. Perfection is what he seeks, not only for
humanity, but for himself. And while he can excuse any
amount of foolishness and fault in the whole of humanity, he
cannot bear it within himself. Or whatever exists inside himself. I think back to that senseless statement I wrote in my
notebook. "If Gene is Star Trek, then Majel is Gene." Other
fragments of memory flood in to surround those words: That
near absence of ego, of selfhood, I detected in Majel so long
ago. Her seemingly irrelevant statement about cutting the
ribbon so it fits. The way she has of looking like she is inhab-
iting her body temporarily, as if her real existence lay somewhere else. That sacrificial "greater love than this has no
one" guillotine posture; that conviction that he is, if not perfect, at least a personal ideal. Somehow in the process of incorporating her into his dreamworld, he became hers. Metaphysically, she has little existence outside of him. And when
he confronts what is left, he does not recognize it. It isn't
perfect. Somehow, they have become dreams to one another.

I think of Spock—how hard it is and how easy it was for
Gene to accept Leonard Nimoy in that role.

Yet when I read Leonard's book, *I Am Not Spock,* I see elements of the same self-identification—evidence of the same
incarnation, echoes of the same conversations. Creator and
created battle in a timeless repetition of Caliban and Setebos,
in an effort to wrest existence out of a dream. The closer one
is to him, the greater expectation he has, and no one is closer
to him than Majel and Spock. In the eighteen months that
follow his death, I talk to his friends. Of the few he calls
intimate friends (all male), all of them see this conundrum. Of
the females, none do. He has been, if not deceptive about his

inner self, at least fiercely protective. He has thrown up a smoke screen, which at times has been interpreted by others, and seemed to say: Majel is not perfect; therefore she does not exist.

When, in the last days of his life, he opens a final door, the smoke clears. He looks at her, a few weeks before he dies, and never takes his eyes from her again.

. • .

It could all be nonsense of course, I think, as I write the passage above. But it isn't. And yet to say more would violate the privacy entrusted to me. No more is necessary, for above this labyrinth of intimacy that lies too deep for tears or answers, they are happy, busy, connected people—separate, together, quarrelsome, peaceful, comfortable, alive. It is only that extension of their passion into a creativity which has so affected the world that makes it significant to any except themselves. Star Trek exists because of both of them.

I remember a conversation we had about his son. At the time, a vital, electrically energetic seventeen-year-old, with a fierce intelligence and dreams of his own, Rod was another source of perfection in his father's eyes. It was during a conversation on anger that the subject came up. "What makes you angry?" I had asked him, and he said, "Nothing." After arguing about that answer for a few minutes, I said, in exasperation, "Well, you have a son. Doesn't he ever make you angry?"

"Oh *no*," Gene says with an unusual vigor. "Of course not. I love him. How could he make me angry? He's perfect." Without accepting this answer, I grow to understand what he means. It is the Rod in his head with whom he is never angry. Happily in this instance the real Rod approximates the dream

The Conversation

boy. There is intense connection between them, and less defi
nition of what perfection means in a son. For Gene, it is
enough that Rod exists, in both worlds. The joy of that existence keeps him from what he defines as anger. But anger
changes definition throughout our conversations. It is a feeling, like fear, that is often cast aside for greater purposes—
like the need to create the world of Star Trek, in which there
is little to be angry about. Later, he admits that as a father, his
children sometimes make him "damned annoyed." But he
laughs as he says it. There is love in his face.

.   •   .

We both become angry once. He has been in a hospital
bed for a week and is almost frantic with this compulsory
restraint. It is almost unendurable to see him lying there, his
head full of wisdom, unable to speak. We visit him several
times a day, and on one of these visits, when Majel leaves the
room to talk to the doctor, he tries to get out of bed. "You
can't do that, Gene," I say. *Star Trek: The Next Generation* is on
the television.

"I can't . . . stay here. Let . . . me . . . up."

"No. I can't. But I'll go get a nurse."

The nurse comes in and tells him to lie down. He asks
why. "You have to stay in bed," she says.

"That's not an answer to *why*," I tell her.

"You have to get well," she tells Gene. He looks furious.
Like a caged lion, he rattles the sides of his bed. "Let me up,"
he says again.

"Now, now. Don't be like that. You have to stay in bed."

He is so outraged, so humiliated by this inane exchange
that he rolls his eyes in my direction like an injured animal.

"Can't you just explain it to him?" I ask.

She doesn't answer. She is essentially a kind person and tucks the covers securely around him. He emits a growl. "There, now," she says, patting him. "You be nice."

I feel his humiliation in a silent game of "Find me." I am enraged, not at her but at the fact that this reality exists. How can he be here, being patronized? It is outrageous.

"You see this TV show?" I point at the screen. "Well this," I point to Gene's shaved and wired head, "is where it came from—every idea, every dream. And *you aren't even speaking to him as a human being.*" I try not to raise my voice. "He isn't an idiot. *Talk to him,* for God's sake. *Explain.* And if you can't, go and get someone who can. This is a *person.* This is an intelligent man."

She looks at my face. "I'll go get a doctor," she says.

I wipe unexpected tears from my face, and sit down.

There is a muffled, weary sound from the bed. "Thanks."

When the doctors arrive, and there are several of them, one asks what the problem is. I explain. He gives Gene a full, complex, and detailed account of his current status, and the reasons it is inadvisable for him to stand upright at this time. "So, you understand," he concludes, "why it is absolutely imperative that you stay put."

"Yes," Gene answers, "I *understand.*"

. • .

He is not as distressed about his inability to speak as others are on his behalf, he tells me later, when he is back home. That communication takes almost a half an hour. "I just . . . think," he says. It seems to be sufficient for the time being. I tell him he is like Stephen Hawking. His face lights up.

"Hero," he says.

Eighteen months later, Stephen Hawking appears on *Star Trek: The Next Generation,* in the episode "Descent," playing himself as a historical figure whose brilliance changed the world. Everyone connected with this episode is honored, awed. Everyone thinks of Gene.

.　●　.

Before all this happens, we talk about male bonding in science fiction. I have just finished writing a series of papers on that theme. This finally leads us to Robert Heinlein's *Space Cadet.*

"I think people in science fiction open their minds—perhaps that's not it—open their consciousness to a lot of relationships," Gene says.

"Perhaps that's because in traditional science fiction, the protagonists are so often not functioning in society. They're on a spaceship or a distant planet, and as they get further and further away from the cultural requirements of their society, they just behave in a more *real* manner. They're the only ones out there, so they rely on each other to supply the human contact and emotional support that would have been spread around and colored by the conventions that no longer exist for them."

"Definitely, that definitely happens. But Bob Heinlein was also capable of creating female bonding—and many other kinds of bonding—and he lived longer than I have in a society which puts limits on how he can think about it. And I am able to think about it a little more broadly, but I am still more limited than, say, some of the people of my acquaintance who have had other experiences. But I have friends that I hug and kiss. I've always been a kisser—or I've always been forming into a kisser and a hugger."

．　●　．

The last time I saw ever Gene, I bent down and gave him a hug, and he took my hand, and kissed it. And the other person with us was very embarrassed. He didn't like that—not comfortable with men holding men. But Gene had no problem with that at all—in public or anywhere, oh no. He was very affectionate.

CHRISTOPHER KNOPF

Gene used to kiss me often after I came back to do *Star Trek: The Next Generation*. And he'd say, "I love you." It made me want to cry. I sensed he didn't have much time left.

ROBERT H. JUSTMAN

．　●　．

"Of course, you grew up in L.A., didn't you?" I say, laughing.

He smiles back. "Yeah, but I also grew up in World War II, in the Pacific and so on."

"Yes," I say doubtfully, wondering in what ways growing up in a war could make one a hugger and kisser. He answers the doubt in my face.

"Well, remember, I grew up into the man who created *Star Trek*."

We both think about this for a while. I wonder out loud if there were Star Trek impulses inherent in his genetic material. He does not think it a fanciful question. Later, when I

learn the circumstances of his birth, I do not think so either.
We both, as children, spent time sitting in grocery boxes dreaming of other worlds. He, some twenty-seven years before me, propelled his grocery box through a thousand galaxies. My destination was more defined: the "when you wish upon a star" star seen each week in what was to me then, and remains now, haunting poignancy, on *The Wonderful World of Disney*. I searched for it every time my mother would allow me to stay outside past dusk, I tell him. "So you too love longing," he remarks, but does not pursue it.

We find out from each other that we would lie awake at night, as very young children, aching with yearning for what we thought of as going *back* to the stars. "I used to cry about it," we tell each other, and in the telling know no more need be said. He piloted real airplanes around the real planet earth, while I was walking home from kindergarten, puzzled by the ever-present horizon, which always seemed like a barrier one was destined to escape. And we muse and reminisce as if we shared the same past, as if we were not a generation, a gender, and a world war apart. Two very new old friends, whose real heroes are fictional characters, and whose lives were both influenced by Robert Heinlein's *Space Cadet*.

"What is it about *Space Cadet* that makes it so important to you?" I ask when we have returned from our shared and separate pasts.

"I think it's just that—bonding. I find that sort of bonding among explorers very compelling. It means so much, has always meant so much to me to know that great science fiction includes great human connection. It speaks to the socio-organism idea that we talked about earlier. *Space Cadet* is a very humane book. It deals with not only the problems of science—about space travel and technology and so on—but of the need we have to act in a conscious responsible manner with all this technology. Of course, it was written many years before space travel was really an actual problem, but the ideas contained within it are timeless. It made a great impression on me."

"Me too. Especially its code, the code the Patrol live by."

"Yes, I know, but I've forgotten exactly what it is. I remember thinking when I was creating *Star Trek,* that our people would have a similar code. 'A band of brothers,' wasn't it?"

.   •   .

In the writers' guide for *Star Trek: The Next Generation,* under the heading "What has not changed" (from the original series), the first item is "The same 'band of brothers' feeling (*and* sisters too, of course!)": "A large part of the success of the original *Star Trek* series is attributable to the fact that it was not a *star and co-star* series, but a *family ensemble* in which the continuing characters felt great affection for each other."

.   •   .

I have *Space Cadet* with me during this discussion, and so read the appropriate passage aloud: " 'I welcome you to our fellowship. You come from many lands, some from other planets. You are of various colors and creeds. Yet you must and shall become a band of brothers.' "

"Yes, that's it," Gene says. "Read the rest."

" 'Some of you are homesick. You need not be. From this day on every part of this family of planets is your home, each place equally.' "

"Each place equally," Gene repeats.

The Conversation

"Each living, thinking creature in this system is your neighbor—and your responsibility.

" 'You are about to take an oath, by your own choice, as a member of the Patrol of this our System. In time, you expect to become an officer of that Patrol. It is necessary that you understand the burden you assume. You expect to spend long hours studying your new profession, acquiring the skills of the spaceman and the arts of the professional soldier. These skills and arts you must have, but they will not make you an officer of the Patrol. . . .

" 'An officer in command of a ship of the Patrol, away from base, is the last of the absolute monarchs, for there is none but himself to restrain him. Many places where he must go no other authority reaches. He himself must embody law, and the rule of reason, justice and mercy.

" 'More than that, to the members of the Patrol singly and together is entrusted such awful force as may compel, or destroy, all other force we know of—and with this trust is laid on them the charge to keep the peace of the System and to protect the liberties of its peoples. They are soldiers of freedom.

" 'It is not enough that you be skillful, clever, brave— The trustees of this awful power must each possess a meticulous sense of honor, self-discipline beyond all ambition, conceit, or avarice, respect for the liberties and dignity of all creatures, and an unyielding will to do justice and give mercy. He must be a true and gentle knight.' "[16]

I look at Gene. "Starfleet," I say.

"Starfleet, yes. That book had such a profound influence on me, as did Bob. There are so many, many ideas that we shared. He wrote many of them down before I did, but they were—have always been in my heart."

"I remember something that you told me early on: that it was a frightening burden to know that you know the answers. Or must find them out for yourself."

"Yes, and that's why I reject religion."

"Yes, and that's why the paper I wrote on *Space Cadet* is subtitled 'The Monastic Journey in Space.' "

"It's not . . . !"

"It is."

"I want to read it."

"Okay."

"Space Cadet is such a significant book for both of us," he says. "Perhaps, in it we meet, in the middle of your strange 'theology'—if that's the right word—and my agnosticism."

"With you staying carefully on your side of the line?"

"For the time being. If I find a different answer, when I have passed on, I'll let you know."

"You'll haunt me?"

"Yes."

.   •   .

He does.

.   •   .

The religious geniuses of all ages have been distinguished by this kind of [cosmic] religious feeling, which knows no dogma and no God conceived in man's image; . . . hence it is precisely among the heretics of every age that we find men who are filled with the highest kind of religious feeling and were in many cases regarded by their contemporaries as Atheists, sometimes also as Saints.

ALBERT EINSTEIN, *THE WORLD AS I SEE IT* (CITADEL PRESS, 1934)

The Conversation

There are a good many contradictions in that Heinlein code. It seems to say: A man (a person) must be everything—a warrior, a pacifist, a staunch individual, and a willing cog in the mechanism of a galactic socio-organism. A man who obeys laws and breaks them, creates his own and polices them. He must be friend to all and to none, because he must be impartial to all. He must walk the line between passion and reason, and never fall, lest he lose his footing forever. He must respect all gods, while honoring his own, renounce his home planet and be at home everywhere. The limits of space are his only boundaries, and the burden of freedom, his only responsibility. And above all, he must be a true and gentle knight.

When in 1993, Gene is posthumously awarded the Robert A. Heinlein Memorial Award for Lifetime Achievement in Promoting the Goal of a Free Spacefaring Civilization, I will write Majel's acceptance speech on behalf of Gene. It is later published in *Ad Astra,* the magazine of the National Space Society. They give it a title: "A True and Gentle Knight."

. ● .

There is another, deeper contradiction in *Space Cadet,* which I have sensed in Gene, and that is the conflict of what it means to him, personally, to be. Throughout our conversations, he has evidenced some distress at his inability to leap beyond the definition of manhood and into the wider realm of personhood. He has been crippled, he tells me once, by his own history as a male person in the twentieth century on Earth. His intimates are men. His heroes are men. And what

Space Cadet is about, beneath its cosmic significance and ontological imperatives, is men, or rather, manhood. Its code, which touches us both on some mysterious symbolic level of the psyche, has something to do with metaphysics for me; for him, I am not sure. I am accustomed, by virtue of my age and particular experience, to investing an idea with a personal relevance, used to reading "person" in place of "man" whenever the substitution is appropriate. *Space Cadet* for me is a book about the human, not gender, spirit.

When I ask Gene about that, though, he makes a potentially explosive observation. He says that it is the virtues of manhood which will carry us into the future, and therefore, they are the virtues he upholds. What he means, of course, is that the attributes traditionally dubbed male—courage, resoluteness, detachment, independence, devotion to duty above personal concerns, a disregard for emotional or physical pain—are the personal qualities that will transport us into the future. He does not need to be told that these traits are the property of humankind, and not just males. But he is at a loss to assimilate them easily and naturally as female attributes in the pattern of life he has led as a male. Something inside him distrusts the reliability of this viewpoint. He has been a man too long.

We have a long, careful conversation about it. He is ashamed to regard himself as parochial, proud that he has not succumbed to the limitations of his own history. He reveals a pattern in this conversation: of monastic detachment, idealism, knighthood, courtly love (the essential ingredient of which is longing), the internal renunciation of the present—in which women richly, fully, properly spend their time—in favor of the future, for which he says he feels responsible. He says, without saying it, that to admit women into his intimate circle is to be seduced into today—that experience is not for him, except momentarily. Apart from Majel, who may travel with him as a dream, he cannot incorporate any bonds within him that bind him to Earth—allow himself any reasons to give up a relentless pursuit of the cause of being, in favor of being it. Women don't understand this, he says. Except, perhaps, nuns. He smiles at me and adds, oddly, mischievously, that he thinks he might like to have been a nun for a while. I dub him Sister Mary Gene. He knows he will be criticized for these statements, asks me to write about rather than transcribe them. Everything makes perfect sense to me. What he says about women is not uncomplimentary. It is his own personal circumstance that drives him from them. They are what they are. As is he.

He talks a lot, during this elliptic conversation, about the fusion and fission of male and female. Somehow, in common with ancient mythologies, he feels that two genders are an evolutionary mistake. When I ask him what the limitations of androgyny are, he cannot answer me.

"What is androgyny exactly?" he asks.

"It means neither male nor female. Both, I guess. Or maybe, not either."

"Well," he says thoughtfully, "I hope I'm not either."

. . .

In his treatment of the Gaan character, Gene describes the world from which he comes. It is called Uhl. "The most significant difference between Uhl and Earth life, perhaps even greater than their life-structure variations, is the ways they replicate themselves. Here too, the early life on Earth and Uhl began in much the same way, with the early organisms of both worlds dividing themselves into identical halves. All life on Uhl still uses variations of that same system, although this world's more complex lifeforms must join into one double-creature and exchange identities before parenthood is possible. Then, upon separating into individuals again, one or both of them are capable of increasing their species population by dividing into replica halves. Each individual gives and shares equally in all this, and any concept of male and female would be meaningless."

·   •   ·

"I've learned to appreciate females very much," Gene goes on. "But I didn't start off appreciating them. I was a writer who believed that men were more logical than women. Now I don't think they're more logical. They may operate on principles of logic more, but I do not consider males mentally superior to women. Physically, perhaps."

"Well, I'd rather have Worf beside me in a fight than Yar—but that may be a failing on my part."

He laughs. "I don't think it's a failing. Worf is a much better security chief. But I am pleased with myself that I have evolved to appreciate women as much as men," he says, looking very pleased with himself indeed. "You see, it's not a matter of superiority or inferiority. It's a kind of difference. Their femaleness is not a sign of weakness—we have very powerful women on *The Next Generation*. But I can't . . . involve Gene Roddenberry in their femaleness. Not in what I have to do. And that is probably a failing on my part."

He mixes metaphysics and sex and gender in a long and complex speech, from which I conclude he means that it is not because he is a man that he feels this way. It is because of the kind of man he is. Quixotic, Questor. Spock. He does not belong here. Nor will he stay much longer. Earth is not really his home.

What *Space Cadet* really means to him is a chance to be a guardian of the human race: an opportunity to live out an ideal in a kind of cosmic monasticism. It is what led me to a place in which *to be* was a true objective; it is what led him to the creation of Star Trek, in which the same objective is implicit. In addition, he has found in *Space Cadet* a manifesto to become a true and gentle knight.

Gentleness is all I have known from Gene. Gentleness and a certain archaic chivalry. At times it seemed at odds with a man whose vision was entirely focused on the future, whose rigorous brain might not leave time for old-fashioned courtesy, and whose friends recount stories of his raucous, bawdy, daredevil exploits. It does not seem consistent with the armor a television producer in Hollywood must inevitably wear. But I never knew his outside personality, never saw him in company for more than a few moments with anyone save his intimates. Perhaps this gentle knight was the result of all his former experience; perhaps he was born that way. When I brought this misgiving to his attention, he was mystified.

"But you are writing about me," he said.

"Yes . . ."

"This is me."

. . .

This is the last long conversation we will have. Tomorrow he will have a stroke. From this point on, we will rely on fragments, referrals to former conversations, individual words. Sometimes, a sentence or two. Tomorrow he begins a new journey.

.   •   .

Sometime in the night, he cries out. He is not well, Majel tells me the next morning. At breakfast, he is unable to articulate clearly. We take him to the doctor. On the way he is patient, smiling, gentle. I wait in the outer office while Majel and Gene are with the doctor. When they emerge, she tells me that he is being sent for a routine scan later that afternoon, and asks me to go with them. Just before that appointment, all the pipes in the house break and there is water everywhere. Majel asks me to take Gene to his second appointment, while she deals with the crisis, and promises to make his favorite dinner. His driver brings the car to the front of the house, and we leave. He will not be back for weeks.

.   •   .

We are sitting in the second doctor's office. We do not speak. Gene's eyes are closed. He leans toward me slightly. "Find me," he whispers. We play our game to distract him from pain. I make up a lot of nonsense, which makes him smile. I know where he is, but am afraid to say it. A receptionist asks him to sign a card. "Just sign your name there," she says. He looks at me with something in his face I do not recognize. He writes nothing. After about a minute, he touches my arm.

"My name?" he asks, politely. I look into his eyes willing it

The Conversation

to be a joke. Horror crawls up my back. My legs begin to
shake. He waits patiently.

"Gene Roddenberry," I say.

"Oh yes. Thank you." I help him write it down, help him back to his seat, and use every ounce of energy I have not to cry. It is not enough. I lower my head. He takes my hand as two tears drop on his beautiful fingers. "Oh," he says, softly, sorrowfully, and closes his fingers. "I'll be alright."

This cannot happen. It can't. He was talking about laser technology yesterday. Eighteen hours ago. I will not believe it. The doctor comes out with a grave face. "Take him to the hospital *now*," he says. "Don't go home. Don't stop anywhere. Just go." He gives me a piece of paper. I call Majel from the car. It is a nightmare; I think I will wake up—it's just the other side of dreams. During the drive to the hospital he says one thing. "I *knew* it."

"Your name?"

"Yes," he says.

"I know you did, Gene. You just couldn't write it."

"Yes," he says. "Thank you."

It is this courteous, courageous, and self-contained demeanor that reveals so much about Gene Roddenberry to me. He is extremely ill. He is in severe pain. He never deviates from his personal code, never once complains. Majel meets us at the hospital, takes care of a thousand details. When it appears that he will have to go into an ambulance to make the short journey from one part of the hospital complex to another, she tells him she will go home—a few blocks away—and get his own things, so he will be more comfortable. "You stay with him," she says, "I'll be back in a few minutes."

In the ambulance we must wait for a while. He holds my

hand and keeps very still. After several moments he tugs at my hand.

"Where's . . . Majel?" he asks.

"She'll be back in a minute."

"Good."

He falls asleep for a few minutes. When he wakes up, he looks at me for a long time.

"I'm afraid," he says.

"I know, Gene."

He grips my hand. "I might die."

"No, I don't think so. Not yet."

He closes his eyes. "Fear," he sighs.

"Yes, I know. The answer to my question."

"Yes."

I stroke his hair with one hand. The other is still in his. "I just don't believe in nothing, Gene."

He smiles again. An odd, brave, grateful smile. "Good."

When he falls into a half sleep again, I wonder where everyone is. It seems as though we have been there for hours. It is, in reality, only a few minutes.

"Majel," he says again, with his eyes still closed.

"Don't worry. She's on her way."

"No—I . . . find me."

I close my eyes, and find him. "That's not what you meant."

"No." He tugs on my hand. "Love her," he says, pulling me closer to him.

"I do."

He is very, very tired, and his next words come with effort. "Never . . . leave . . . her."

I bite my lip until it bleeds. "No, of course not. Don't

worry." I want so badly to pretend that I feel he is not dying.
But I am not an actress after all. Not with him. He kisses my
hand and falls asleep.

Majel arrives a few minutes later, takes one look at my face
and pinches me on the arm, hard. "He is going to be FINE,"
she hisses. "Now *look* like it." She lets my arm go with a
warning glance as he wakes up and sees her. He seeks her
eyes for signs of his existence. The look on his face is akin to
ecstasy. He opens his arms.

"Well, my darling," she says to Gene, cupping his face with
her hands and kissing him. "What have you two been up
to—to get yourselves into this situation?!"

. . .

Only a few days before, in that discussion about acting,
Gene had asked me to tell him what I thought was the best
performance I had ever seen a *Star Trek* actor give. This was it.

. . .

He lives for a few more weeks. During those weeks, we
visit him in the hospital, make lists of words he can point to
when he cannot speak, take him out to dinner when he is
well enough to come home. He has no trouble thinking. We
talk a little. One day he seems much better. He speaks in
sentences.

"I'm sorry about the book," he says.

"Never mind," I tell him. "We'll get back to it when you're
better." I feel I am being false, but Majel is nearby, and I do
not wish to be pinched again. He looks at me steadily and

knowingly. He has seen me look at him where he is, slightly adrift of his body, which now has a translucent quality I recognize from past experience.

"I have to die, you know," he says when Majel is out of earshot.

I do not answer him.

"I'm not afraid, now." He looks toward the door. "Take care of her. She doesn't understand . . ."

"I know. I will."

"Promise?"

I nod my head. How assiduously they protect each other. There will be no "until death do us part."

"Go to the set. Find me."

"Gene . . ."

He will not listen. He gives me instructions all day long.

Just before I leave to go home, I go into the bedroom to say goodbye. I embrace the fragile body in which there once lived a six-foot-three L.A. cop, a Pan Am pilot, a World War II hero, a Hollywood television producer, a legend, a mystic, a friend—and in which he is now barely present. "Come back often," he says. "Come back *soon*." As I walk out the door, he says, "I love you."

I never see him again.

s there a portrait of Gene Roddenberry in all this? There might be. It depends on the viewer. To those for whom a portrait is an interpretation, a few lines sketched in the brief passage of the time between life and death, between substance and shadow, yes. To those who expect a photographic likeness, no, there is no portrait. The light will always be wrong, the profile not sharp enough, the shutter speed not quick enough to catch the face of a man who turns suddenly to the window to catch a glimpse of an undiscovered star.

One will always wonder if he is the man at the Harvard lectern, discoursing on the future of photo-electric cells, or the man who dissects the symbology of acting, all the while playing happily with the cast of characters inside himself—becoming first one, then another—in order to discover what it means "to be." He is too quick for the artist's brush, too still for the movie camera, which seeks a few seconds' sum-mary in the face of the unknown. Was he human? Yes. As human as every alien he created. Did he ever feel a part of humanity? No. He felt as alien as every human who walks this earth in his shell of flesh: "self-contained, separate . . . terribly lonely."[1]

       .   ●   .

The first day I met him, I asked him what one sentence he would like for an epitaph. Without hesitation, he replied, "He loved humanity."

       .   ●   .

And yet, when I look back, there was one evening in June, when the world seemed to open up for a few seconds as Majel passed by. He looked at her, and then his eyes traveled to the purple evening sky. "You know, Yvonne," he said with a kind of awe in his voice, "if I could just understand Majel, I think I could understand the whole of humanity."

The phenomenon of Star Trek owes its existence to Gene Roddenberry, creator, writer, producer, visionary, and catalyst of the future. Gene Roddenberry was a man of dreams who talked with presidents, astronauts, physicists, and scholars, but listened to fans. He held a universe in his head called "the future"—a place not devoid of danger (for he was a courageous man) but a place of essential peace, full of wonders yet unknown, where it was possible for the human race to grow. He named it Star Trek.

. • .

For every television show there is an audience, whether it numbers one hundred or one million. In the case of *Star Trek* and *Star Trek: The Next Generation* the numbers are virtually uncountable, not because there are no statistics but because Star Trek is more than a television show. It is also the philosophy expressed through it.[1]

Gene Roddenberry loved ideas—and he loved people. He believed until the day he died in the essential goodness of humanity. "If there was one theme in all of Star Trek," he said, "it was that the glory of our universe is its infinite combinations of diversity. That all beauty comes out of diversity. What a terrible, boring world it would be if everyone agreed with everyone else. When we are truly wise—and my test for a wise human is when they take a positive delight when someone says 'I disagree with you because . . .'—my God, what an opportunity will open!"

. • .

When the Smithsonian Institution mounted a Star Trek exhibition in the National Air and Space Museum in 1992, it was acknowledging what millions of people have known for years: Star Trek is a significant influence in American culture. It is a legend, an adventure, a philosophy, a dream.

Star Trek has been absorbed into American culture gradually since 1966. The original television series, *Star Trek*, premiered on September 8, 1966, and was canceled three years later; *Star Trek: The Next Generation* began in 1986 and is as of this writing in its seventh season; and *Star Trek: Deep Space Nine* continues the legacy of Star Trek, although it is not Gene Roddenberry's original creation. The success of the television series has inspired seven movies, featuring the original cast and the cast of *The Next Generation,* and twenty-two animated *Star Trek* episodes. The Star Trek universe, as it is popularly known, now comprises all of these, as well as a series of clubs, organizations, fanzines, merchandise, conventions, monthly mass market publications, novels, official fan club magazines, serious studies examining the meaning of each episode, technical manuals, and much more.

At first, Star Trek devotees were dubbed a subculture by
the media. That is no longer true. Nor is it true that all devotees are "Trekkies," or "Trekkers," as they prefer to be called. Gene Roddenberry's *Star Trek* was and is watched and admired by business, education, and religious leaders, by scientists, astronomers, astronauts, professors, teachers, corporate executives, artists, musicians, writers, doctors, parents, students, children, and government leaders, including presidents of the United States.

. • .

Because of Gene Roddenberry's unprecedented insistence that there be a black female officer on the bridge of the starship *Enterprise,* you may have heard Dr. Martin Luther King Jr.'s comment on *Star Trek* to Nichelle Nichols (Lieutenant Uhura on the original series): "You have opened a door that can never be closed again. Because of you and the way you portray the character, people will see us. The world will see us as we should be seen—men and women on an equal basis going where no one has gone before."

. • .

If you thumb through a few university catalogues, you will see among the philosophy and English classes, several on Star Trek. From the early 1970s to the early 1990s, you would have had the opportunity to hear Gene Roddenberry lecture at almost every major and many minor universities in America. Your computer may have been designed by a *Star Trek* fan of twenty years ago, who was inspired by the voice-activated computer on the *Enterprise* and decided to enter the future. Your doctor may have been moved to go into medicine by the character of Dr. McCoy. Your neighbor, son, daughter, brother, sister, parent, or friend may have been encouraged, not to follow a particular profession represented on the program, but to explore his or her own talents and develop them to the private, particular, internal standard of satisfaction that *Star Trek* advocates. If you have seen the first U.S. space shuttle, you've seen the precursor of a starship that isn't built yet, for people from around the country wrote to President Ford to ask that the test shuttle be named *Enterprise.*[2]

. . .

Star Trek is not just the property of America. It is a global commodity. Seen in over two hundred countries, translated into over forty languages, it is now an influence on planet Earth that cannot be ignored. In England you may open a British telephone book and find an advertisement encouraging businesses to print their names in bold type. It reads: **Boldly Go** and cites an example, KIRK, ADMIRAL, JAMES T. SPC. EXPLR, adding that every enterprise needs a little assistance. No picture of the *Enterprise,* no logo, no Spock. Throughout the world it is assumed that a reference to Star Trek will be understood.

. . .

Walking through a toy store, you will inevitably come upon action figures, model ships, and communicators, all from the *Star Trek* series. It is virtually impossible to avoid the hundreds of Star Trek items available elsewhere—from uniform patterns to sweatshirts to mugs. Art galleries across the country now display a new genre that has come to be known as Star Trek art. And if computers are part of your life, there is a surprising array of Star Trek software to be found, from games to screen savers to educational programs. If you prefer to browse quietly through a bookstore, you will find shelves of Star Trek books, from novels (Pocket Books publishes one a month and to date has sold over 26 million copies, making its series the best selling in publishing history) to technical manuals that specify the physical properties and propulsion systems of the *Enterprise.*

.   •   .

If you are not "into" science fiction, and prefer the more spiritual pursuits of Eastern philosophy, you might have had to wait patiently on the set of *Star Trek: The Next Generation* with monks from the Dalai Lama's monastery in India as they watched, transfixed, their spiritual leader's favorite television show come to life.

.   •   .

These are but a few of the ways in which you may have become acquainted with Star Trek, simply by living in the twentieth century. And at the heart of this phenomenon lies the real Star Trek: its creator.

At the death of Gene Roddenberry in 1991, boxes of mail from around the world were delivered for months to his widow, Majel Barrett Roddenberry. Every letter said the same thing: "Star Trek changed my life." It is perhaps the wondrous *personal* future Star Trek represents—its celebration of the human journey, its belief in the human spirit, and its message of love and tolerance for all life forms—that remains unequaled by any television program today.

. • .

You may not have watched *Star Trek* on television, but if you have been to NASA or seen a space shuttle flight or used a cellular telephone, you will have encountered it in real life. Many scientists, astronauts, and engineers attribute their inspiration, perseverance, and success to the influence of *Star Trek*. You have experienced it if you have been in the hospital recently, where medical computers monitor life functions, a direct result of the "bio-comps" first seen on *Star Trek*. If you have seen the *Emmy Awards, Saturday Night Live, David Letterman,* or *Wonder Years,* a commercial for Tazers, or any number of television shows that make reference to the inheritance of Star Trek as a cultural phenomenon, you have felt its presence. Or perhaps, catching the tail end of a "real-life" police show while waiting for the evening news, you may have seen a policeman make an arrest, as I did one evening: "Where's your partner?" he asked. "Here," the suspect replied. "Whaddya mean, here?" the policeman demanded. "He was on the other side of town a couple of minutes ago. What did he do? Beam down from the *Enterprise?"*

In the Smithsonian Institution you may have seen a mythic starship, permanently displayed as though it existed, next to Orville and Wilbur Wright's historic biplane and Charles Lindbergh's *Spirit of St. Louis*. If you were there in 1992, you would have seen that Star Trek exhibition—a display of what has come to be known as contemporary American mythology—which increased visitation by 25 percent in the year it was there. And, had you been quick enough to purchase tickets in the first few hours of their availability, you could have attended a symposium on the significance of Star Trek in Washington, D.C., the same year.

If you walk down Hollywood Boulevard, there will be, among the sidewalk stars of the screen giants of U.S. film culture, one named Gene Roddenberry, the first writer ever to be so honored. And if you are, like him, a person whose eyes are drawn magnetically to the night sky, then you may see among the billions of stars in the cosmos one called Roddenberry, so designated in memory of a man who spent his life trying to reach them.

·   •   ·

If you *view* the original *Star Trek* series, you will notice a lot of orange paint, plastic plants, a pointy-eared guy named Spock, and a collection of rubbery aliens. If you *see* it, you will encounter questions, and very few answers: How can we overcome prejudice? What is death? Should we orchestrate war? Is patriotism a disease? What is the difference between sexuality and love? When does duty end and morality begin? Should there be government? Whose ethics predominate in a relationship—mine or yours? And most often: What does it mean to be human?

If you *view* the series *Star Trek: The Next Generation,* you will notice great special effects, terrific makeup, and astounding technology. If you *see* it, you will encounter the same questions, explored in greater detail, with additional concerns that our current society engenders: Do machines live? What use is religion? Is love the exclusive property of heterosexuals? Just because we can do something, should we? What is the difference between dreams and reality? What is consciousness? Is there a case for drug dependency? What is the difference between male and female power? Are ethics morals? And again, most often: What does it mean to be human?

And if it seems silly to expect so much from a commercial television show, you may be surprised to find out that Gene Roddenberry agreed with you. But he expected it of *Star Trek* anyway.

.　●　.

There is one other thing. If you watch *Star Trek*, look for yourself. You will be there.

The Conversation

1.   The phrase is that of Gene's friend, Robert Jastrow, from *Red Giants and White Dwarfs*.

2.   After Gene died, Majel and I went through boxes and boxes of his papers. The socio-organism papers were never found. They were among many items that were discovered to be missing in the days following Gene's death.

3.   Gene did not write the episode "Q Who." The connection is mine. And yet, somehow, this illustrates the value of the Star Trek philosophy, for out of the thousands of scripts that could have been made into episodes, few were chosen to be incorporated into the thinking world that *Star Trek* represents. What is engendered from an original seed is a population of ideas, each of which forms a cell in the philosophical organism which once consisted of only one man: Gene Roddenberry.

4. Part of a corporate mind/entity/race called the Q Continuum, Q is one manifestation of his species. He is a being or state of being (or beings) that we never quite comprehend. *The* Q are among the most fascinating aliens that Gene Roddenberry created. Charming, insincere, manipulative, callous, Q is so often infuriating—and so often right. We dislike him (most of the time), we fear him (some of the time), we are angered, even outraged by him (nearly all of the time) and yet, despite ourselves, we look forward to Q's arrival because we learn a little more about ourselves from him. From the episode "Encounter at Farpoint" through various escapades and incidents, he continues to baffle, annoy, endanger, confound, and enrage us, and yet his antics are curiously ineffectual. In the end, despite all he can do, we remain standing. Q never really defeats us, because he somehow seems to need us—or perhaps because he never really understands us. Our humanity is our defense, even as Q's presence requires us to reexamine what it means to be human and mortal.

5. "The Enemy Within," a first-season episode of *Star Trek,* the original series, is a classic study of good and evil within oneself. When a transporter malfunction causes Captain Kirk to be beamed aboard the *Enterprise* in duplicate, one intelligent and compassionate, the other amoral and dominated by primal urges, we see one of Gene Roddenberry's most fundamental concerns: the synthesis between the animal brain and the forebrain, which he believed was essential to the evolution of the human race. Most significant in this episode is the attribution of "good" characteristics inherent in the "bad" persona of Kirk, and the reverse. The ability to dissect morality—to examine by implication and logic the

fundament of right and wrong at the point of origin and/or coexistence—was one of Gene's most rigorous pursuits, and one with which he unceasingly turned to Hitler as a study of the human organism.

6. The desire to merge, to unify, to become one with another being has always been a part of the passionate human existence. More than just an insurance of the continuance of the species, our deepest connections reach beyond the mere physical, into the depths of the mind, psyche, and spirit. Union—in myriad forms and for myriad reasons—is not merely a recurring theme in *Star Trek*: it is a raison d'être. Gene Roddenberry was fascinated with the variety and depth of attraction and connection between humans and other beings and the endless number of ways in which one being can bond with another, each one of which can be called "love." Transcending race, gender, creed, appearance, and ideology, Star Trek purports that love in all forms is something to be celebrated, not feared. In this incredible scene the merging of man and machine is spellbinding. V-ger's mechanical probe, Ilia, and the human Commander Decker begin the spectacular journey into oneness that will create a new lifeform. From its rich palette of emotional, physical, and mental experience, Star Trek manifests its own credo: Infinite diversity in infinite combinations.

7. The Bynars appear in "1001001," an episode of *Star Trek: The Next Generation*. They are a benevolent race, so integrated with computers that they operate in pairs and speak a binary language. The Trills are symbiant beings, composed of a humanoid host body and a highly intelligent sluglike creature that lives in the torso of the host; this long-lived parasitic creature may inhabit several different hosts during

its lifespan. In the episode "The Host," Dr. Beverly Crusher falls in love with a Trill, who is fatally injured and whose parasitic component must be transferred temporarily to Commander Riker, a "brotherly" friend, while awaiting a new host. Dr. Crusher finds herself still in love with the inner being, now within a man she regards as a brother. The question of what it is that we love inside someone is brought to a stunning conclusion when the new host arrives—*a woman.* The nature of love and sexuality is deeply explored in this provocative study of human emotion.

8. I write this only for the record, because what followed is something I promised Gene to say only to Leonard Nimoy. I have said it. And in any case, it does not belong to the province of this book. What is important here is Gene's insistence on the separation of his Spock and Leonard Nimoy's Spock, and his equal tenacity in holding fatherly love for a man with whom he once shared his creation. For among the very many people Gene Roddenberry knew, few were able to enter that cosmic Oz with him—his own private universe where once he found Spock, and once took Leonard Nimoy to meet him.

9. These conversations were never found. Gene's illness prevented him from looking for them, and although we conducted a thorough search of his private files after his death, these papers, among others, remain missing to this day.

10. The three laws of robotics are: (1) A robot may not injure a human being, or, through inaction, allow a human being to come to harm; (2) A robot must obey the orders given it by human beings, except where such orders would conflict with the First Law; and (3) A robot must protect its existence, as long as such protection does not conflict with

the First or Second Laws (From Isaac Asimov, *I, Robot* [Doubleday, 1950]).

11. Since this conversation, there have been several episodes that outline the Riker/Troi relationship more clearly, according to Gene's original plan.

12. IDIC refers to "Infinite Diversity in Infinite Combinations," the central principle around which the Star Trek universe is constructed. It is symbolized by a Vulcan ornament that Spock wears, seen in the episode "Is There in Truth No Beauty?" The IDIC ornament has been made into earrings, pins, and pendants, and is worn by many *Star Trek* fans as a tribute to the ideal of universal tolerance for all life forms.

13. It doesn't seem possible that I had known Gene for several months before meeting Ernie. In the last days of Gene's life, no one prolongs it with more care than this tender, faithful, freedom-giving man whom Gene does not want to lose. We have been friends now for longer than I knew Gene. Ernie is now Majel's personal assistant. I am grateful for his many selfless acts, which epitomize what Gene meant by those three words in "The City on the Edge of Forever": Let me help. Ernie was, and remains today, a constant reminder of the fact that Gene practiced what he preached: chose to have in his private life and home only those in whom a certain Star Trek quality was present—and in whom the distance between philosophy and reality was easily traversed in order to facilitate the manifestation of his dreamworld.

14. In this episode, a group of miners on the planet Janus VI are being systematically killed by what they perceive as a monster. The *Enterprise* is called in to hunt down the creature,

which is a silicon-based life form that can burrow through stone. Spock, however, joins minds (mind-melds) with the alien, the Horta, and discovers that it is an intelligent life form, a mother who was killing to protect her unborn children nestled in the silicon nodules (eggs) the miners were destroying. Kirk negotiates a symbiotic agreement between the Horta and the miners. She and her children will burrow through the mine (they ingest rock for nourishment) for the miners, who promise to leave them in peace. The underlying theme of this study of xenophobia is the exploration of being—each other.

15.   Warp drive is a delicately balanced, intricate web of chemistry, physics, mathematics, and mystery. Although various members of the *Enterprise* crew seem to understand it, our experience with the Traveller in "Where No One Has Gone Before" demonstrates that true understanding of something comes only with the ability to create it. Basically, warp drive involves the bending, or warping, of space to allow two stationary points to become closer to each other. Although measured in terms of the speed of light, warp drive has more to do with energy than speed. According to the *Star Trek Writers' Technical Manual,* Warp 1 equals the speed of light, and no ship can exceed Warp 10, which is the absolute limit of the universe. In other words, at Warp 10 all points in the universe occupy the same timespace; or, as the manual puts it, "an object at that 'speed' would occupy all points in the universe simultaneously." The warp factor scale is "asymptotic," which means that Warp 4 is over twice the "speed" of Warp 3. The normal cruising speed of the *Enterprise* in deep space is Warp 6, about 326 times the speed of light.

16.   Robert Heinlein, *Space Cadet* (Random House, 1948), pp. 45–46.

1.   Spock/Kolos in "Is There in Truth No Beauty?" *Star Trek,* the original series, third season.

Appendix: About Star Trek

1.   Following convention, I have throughout this book used *Star Trek* to refer to the television programs, both the original series (1966–69) and *Star Trek: The Next Generation* (1986–). Star Trek, without italics, refers to the philosophy Gene Roddenberry incorporated in his work and to the cultural phenomenon his work engendered.

2.   This was not the first time such letter-writing energy by *Star Trek* fans had had such influence. Eight years earlier, in 1968, when NBC was going to cancel *Star Trek* after only two seasons, an overwhelming barrage of protest mail persuaded the reluctant network to renew it for a third season.

Acknowledgments

To the luminous, the loving, the helpful, the courageous; to the dispossessed and longing; to the mis-
taken, the empathic, the gifted, the unready; to the
practiced, courageous, and afraid; to the friends, colleagues,
and heroes; to the fans whom Gene loved—and to the serendipitous messengers, for their help in the preparation of this
book, I am grateful. They know who they are.

Majel Barrett Roddenberry	Arthur C. Clarke
Ernest C. Over	E. Jack Neuman
Robert H. Justman	Sam Rolfe
Christopher Knopf	William Ware Theiss

Lawrence Lowry, Christopher J. Terry, John Geoffrey Harri-
son, William J. McClung, Edward Snow, Brandon Tartikoff,
Christopher C. H. Simmons, Richard E. A. Simmons, Isaac
Asimov, Janet Asimov, Doug Abrams Arava, Gladys An-

228 donian, Spock, Richard F. Fern, E. J. Fern, William E. Haynes, Patricia Everson, Alan Bernard, Angelo and Pat Scaramastra, Camille Paglia, Mort Zarkov, Rod Roddenberry, Issamu, Louis Rosner, Madeline Riley, Shirley Maiewski, Marta Houske, Charles Musès, Leonard Nimoy, several friends of Gene who wish to remain anonymous, Barbara Marx Hubbard, Matt Dodson, Ray Bradbury, Robert Heinlein, James Clarke, Wilton Dillon, Robert Jastrow, Sallie Baliunas, the casts and crews of *Star Trek* and *Star Trek: The Next Generation,* the University of California Press, Amy Einsohn, Russell Galen.

.   •   .

Those whom I must thank most for their sensitivity and generosity, I can thank least, as is always the case. It is the fact that they exist on this planet for which I am wondrously grateful:
Bill, an intimate of dreamworlds.
Majel, about whom nothing adequate can be said.
Ernie, whom I should not like to lose.
Bob, among other things, for his comment on Satyajit Ray.
My parents, who know why.
My children, who will.

Above all, and in all ways, A. C. Crouch
Semper eadem

The exploration of space is one of humanity's most astounding achievements. It was also Gene Roddenberry's greatest dream. Don't let Gene's dream die.

PLEASE SUPPORT OUR SPACE PROGRAM.

Write to Spacecause * 922 Pennsylvania Avenue * Washington DC 20003 * or call (202) 543-1900

Designer:	Steve Renick
Compositor:	ComCom
Text:	Monotype Columbus & Monotype Perpetua
Display:	Monotype Perpetua
Printer:	Haddon Craftsmen, Inc.
Binder:	Haddon Craftsmen, Inc.